The personal life story of Maureen McKenna and her husband Hugh has been for me a window into both the heart of God and his power to change lives. This book confirms in vivid and dramatic reality what I have come to know of God through my dear friends.

Laspic Stewart,
Chairman, Open Door Trust Glasgow

Once, like us all, a prisoner of sin, Maureen McKenna is set free by the Lord Jesus to do what is right. She and her husband Hugh, now reach others who are still trapped. And what is it people hear Maureen say? It's the thrill in her voice as she tells people, 'I just love the Lord Jesus'. This is a compelling book. Let's pray with Maureen, Hugh, and the volunteers at Open Door Trust Glasgow, that many more may be set free to proclaim the good news, as Maureen does.

Rev Jackie Ross,
President, Blythswood International

Descend into a deep, dark and cold underworld lit only by a long line of lamps God has placed there to guide the traveller through lonely regions. The names on many lamps are familiar – Mother Teresa, Mary Slessor, Eric Liddell. But wait. Here is a new lamp and amazingly under it the sound of laughter and praise. Read on – join the praise of a God who called us out of darkness into his marvellous light.

Alan Devereux, member of the Board of
Open Door Trust Glasgow

'In this book Maureen McKenna tells of her early life and how she met Jesus, who gave her peace and a fresh start. However, the main thrust of the book is about the work that Maureen, her husband Hugh, and others have done, and are still doing, in the more sleazy parts of Glasgow, among those who appear to have no hope - the homeless, alcoholics, prostitutes, drug addicts, criminals recently released from prison, and many others. Maureen believes that her faith must be demonstrated in good works. Like the Apostle James, she is in no doubt that a 'faith without works is dead'. This is a challenging book which should encourage Christians to get out into the market place and share their faith and works with those most in need.

Sir David McNee,
Retired Commissioner of Police of the Metropolis

Maureen McKenna's life story breathes the air of the two worlds in which she has lived. The Glasgow in which she was born and whose people she so obviously loves, and the Kingdom of God whose transforming power has made her the remarkable woman she has become. Those who know Maureen will hear her voice on every page of the narrative; most others will feel, when they come to the last page, that she has become a personal friend. *Whitewashed Stairs to Heaven* tells a story of great need. But it also describes an even greater love, displayed in all kinds of unexpected and surprising ways. Maureen McKenna is an ordinary woman made extraordinary by God's grace. Here is the challenging and inspiring story of someone prepared to exhaust herself loving God and serving others. A great read!

Rev Sinclair Ferguson,
St George's Tron Church, Glasgow

WHITEWASHED STAIRS TO HEAVEN

Maureen McKenna and the 'Open Door Trust Glasgow'

Maureen McKenna with Irene Howat

Christian Focus Publications

Copyright © 2000 Christian Focus Publications
ISBN 1-85792-616-1

Published in 2000
by
Christian Focus Publications, Geanies House, Fearn,
Ross-shire, IV20 1TW, Scotland, Great Britain

www.christianfocus.com

Printed and bound in Great Britain by
Cox & Wyman, Reading, Berkshire

Cover design by Owen Daily

Cover photograph supplied by Springburn Museum
Trust, Atlas Square, Ayr Street, Glasgow, G21 4BW

Contents

Dedication

For Hugh, my mentor and best friend, and for Paul, our son, our miracle. And in loving memory of my brother John, and of those we have known and loved whilst working on the streets of Glasgow who have died in tragic circumstances.

Foreword

Maureen McKenna's story is, in its way, a gripping piece of travel-writing. Not that she describes far-off continents or islands. Instead, she has lived and worked in that unknown world that lurks behind the glitz and glamour of our city streets. It is there, in what a recent writer calls the 'Dark Heart' of our society, that she herself discovered the life-changing reality of Jesus Christ. And it is there that she and her husband, Hugh, have brought true light into the dark lives of prostitutes and addicts and all the other sad, abandoned and abused people they have met. For many, reading this book will be a journey into places and situations they never knew existed. It will challenge the glib judgements and the too-ready condemnations that are often passed on the citizens of that dark realm. And it will surely give tremendous encouragement to many to imitate the McKennas' work in other cities and towns throughout the world.

Most of all, the book is stirring evidence that, however dark and hidden that world appears to us, God's power and love can shine even there. Government policies and urban renewal schemes can change the environment, fund organisations, and create opportunities. But only God can change people. And he does. If you doubt that, read on!

John Nicholls
Director of Recruitment and Training
London City Mission

Acknowledgements

There are so many people without whom this book would never have been written because there would be no story to tell. I owe each of them my thanks. The Chairman and Board of Trustees have support me with their love and wisdom. Our wonderful volunteers, who have given unstintingly of their time and gifts, have enriched my life. Churches, schools and individuals throughout Glasgow and beyond, have been involved in our work for over fifteen years. Our mothers and families have always been there for us when we needed them. Friends, Robert, May and family, walked every step of the way with us as we embarked on our new venture. My precious husband, Hugh, who entered my hurting world has walked gently beside me, upholding me. His unconditional love, understanding and encouragement has marked our life together. Through Hugh, I met my Saviour Jesus, and my life was changed. Our dear son Paul, has generously shared his dad and mum with many others, and he has made our lives complete. Irene Howat, who helped me write this book, shared my joys, my tears and my innermost thoughts. Our time together was very special and we have become firm friends. Finally, I want to thank Margaret Taylor, whose life and commitment to the work of the Trust has been a source of joy and encouragement to all of us. I wish to thank them all from the bottom of my heart.

Introduction

My greatest desire in sharing my life and the work God has called me to do, is that it will in some way give hope to those who are broken by life's circumstances and who can see no way ahead and no future.

It is my prayer that this book will help break down barriers and prejudices regarding those on the perimeter of society whose social and spiritual needs are so great. May God grant that my experiences will encourage others who are reaching out in their own communities, but who fear the task is to big and too difficult. I have found God to be able and faithful.

As I have looked back over my life I have been challenged afresh to be salt and light in this needy world. I hold that challenge out to all who read this book.

1

The centre of the world

McAslin Street was the centre of the world. Moving out from the street took the adventurer to Townhead in the east end of Glasgow. But for most of us most of the time there was no need for such bravado, for McAslin Street was the centre of the world.

'They're looking down at us,' Jean said, pointing up to the row of tenement windows that overlooked the back court, each like an eye glinting in the afternoon sunshine. 'Even when there's nobody there the windows keep an eye on us,' she concluded.

'They won't see us if we go to the doctor's,' I suggested tentatively.

Jean looked around, There were other children about but none were watching us. 'Come on then,' she urged. 'Run for it!'

Without a backward glance, we made our bid for privacy. A quick sprint brought us to the doctor's wall. Within the minute we had shimmied up and over, only stopping for the briefest space of time to check no-one was around and to brace ourselves for the drop on the other side.

And there it was. The doctor's garden. Beauty and privacy was ours for the borrowing provided nobody knew we were there. Keeping a weather eye on the back of the doctor's house for any movement, we headed between the flower beds to the oak tree, from one of whose branches hung a rope swing. Then it was shots each. It didn't matter when it was not my turn for the alternative to swinging was just as enjoyable. While Jean swung, I lay on the grass under the oak tree dreaming. And when my turn came, my imagination soared with the swing.

'I'm going to have a garden just like this,' I informed my friend.

She opened one eye and squinted at me through the sunlight, 'Are you?' she asked. 'And where's the money going to come from?'

'I'll work for it,' said I. 'And I'll buy things you see in American films. You just wait. And you can come and visit me and we'll take our tea out into the garden. It will be just like this,' I went on, 'with flowers and trees and a swing.'

But Jean's eyes were closed. I didn't know what she was dreaming about, but I knew my dreams through and through. I would better myself. I wouldn't always live in McAslin Street. I wouldn't always have to climb the wall into the doctor's garden to find privacy. One day I would have a room of my own in a house of my own with a garden all of my very own. Of such things were my dreams made. But, unlike Jean, my dreams were woven when I was wide awake and they centred on a world beyond my own, on a world beyond McAslin Street. Sometimes, just sometimes, snippets from my dream world descended into the street. But they had more to do with my vivid imagination than with hard reality.

And reality was hard. Alcoholism was rife along the one and a half miles of the street, and it brought its usual devastation in its wake. Many families lived on the bread line. Wives scrimped and scraped to gather enough to feed their families, the best always going to the 'old man' who was sometimes too drunk even to know what he was eating, and what was left when everyone else had finished was what they ate. Many a child there was who thought Mum didn't like meat, for he so rarely saw her eat it. While I saw that happen round about me, I knew there would be a meal on our table. Our mum was different.

Brought up in Henngoyd Garden Village in Wales, Mum met Dad during the war when she was a cook, and a lance corporal, in the army. He was from Glasgow, and that was where they made their home. Mum's skill as a wartime cook stood her in good stead when the three of us came along. John, my older brother by a year, and Brian who is nine years younger than me, and I never went hungry. Even though times were hard, Mum could always make a meal to fill us. Sometimes after teatime there would be a knock at the door.

'Can we empty the bin for you, Mrs. McKenna?' one of the two little girls at the door would ask.

Mum kept a pail of garbage in the kitchen for them to take down to the midden in the back court.

Looking out the window, with my comfortably full stomach, I watched as the girls scrapped over the crumbs in the cereal packet and the sauce at the bottom of the baked beans' tin. Seeing them fight over what we had thrown out confirmed me in my determination. No child of mine would fight over food from someone else's rubbish bin. That, to me, was poverty. So was going without shoes. Sometimes I had to wear wellington boots until Mum could buy me shoes. That was a pity but it wasn't poverty. At least I had my wellies.

I suppose how we got our Friday night tea was a sign of financial hardship, but for me it was the treat of the week. After school I ran up the stairs to the house, pushing the door open knowing I'd be welcomed with the smell of cleanness. Friday was the day Mum disinfected everything. The red linoleum in the kitchen shone from her hard work, and the hearth rug, the only carpeting we had, lay in front of a roaring fire for Friday was the day the coalman came. And it was pay night, and that to the young McKennas meant fish and chips and Irn Bru. Every week our downstairs neighbour lent us the money to buy our meal knowing she'd get it back when Dad came in with his wages. We were sent to Mrs. Nimmo with a note written on brown paper. Mrs. Nimmo would read it, wrap the requested coins in the paper, then send it and us back upstairs. An excited race to the chip shop followed, and I can still smell the warm vinegary aroma of the newspaper wrapped package we carried home. With our fish, chips and Irn Bru we felt richer than royalty.

Friday night was also entertainment night. Mums leant out their windows, leaning on pillows with decent pillowcases (that was important, we had standards) and watched the world go by. Having been brought up in a cottage in a Welsh village, this tradition was one that Mum had to learn. By the time I was old enough to notice, she was very much part of the conversation that was batted from window to window and across the street. As time wore on, the menfolk straggled home from the pub. It seemed to me that there were three ways they could come home, either bouncy, staggering or crawling. 'Is that no' terrible,' one woman would comment on a man crawling along the street. 'He's got five weans and he's drunk a' his wages.' And one embarrassed and distressed wife would take her pillow off the windowsill and go in to wait for whatever was to come.

But there was cosiness too. In my younger years I slept in the recess bed in the kitchen. This was a nest fit for Goldilocks, thick and plumpy. In the winter I had the benefit of the black grate fire which was banked up with dross then damped down to see it through the night. When Dad and Mum went off to bed, there would still be little flickers of firelight to stimulate my imagination. They seemed to me to create a world of ballerinas spinning and pirouetting around the walls of the room. It was then I went into my upside down world, my last thing at night before I went to sleep world. Lying there in the near darkness, I imagined what it would be like to live in a world that was all upside down, where people walked on ceilings and lights swung from the floor, where curtains hung up the way and water from the tap ran up the way too. When the world upset me, I turned it upside down for comfort. When all was well, I did it just for fun.

'I'm bored,' I hear youngsters say from the midst of all their educational toys, battery operated whatsits and computer games. They know nothing of the delights of McAslin Street. We skipped using old clothes rope, played hide and seek in the closes and backcourts, kicked cans along the street making a fine din in the process, and spent endless hours playing two balls against a wall in any number of singing games. Singing was a feature of the street. We had so little, youngsters now have so much, yet I can't remember when I last heard a child outside playing a game and singing to himself.

And there were our toys. My friends and I sat on the stairs looping coloured elastic bands together so that we could play Chinese ropes. For the uninitiated, these were attached to two sets of ankles, one opposite the other. What fun we had making designs with them, and what acrobatic positions we got into. But, most exciting of all, were bogeys. An orange box, some odd bits of wood, discarded pram wheels and a length of old clothes rope could be built into a bogey which gave month after month of pleasure. And there were refinements in the art of bogey building. Tin tops off beer bottles, scavenged from rubbish bins outside the local public houses, were hammered into the orange crates in a variety of designs. The more bottle tops, the greater the kudos. And that kind of kudos mattered in a street in which sixty or seventy children could be seen out playing at one time. That being the case, imagine how I felt when Mum bought me my very own ball bearing roller skates on which I just flew over the shiny cobbled surface of our part of the street!

Not all of our activities were as legitimate. In the four storey tenement blocks the doors of flats faced each other on each of the stair landings. They just asked to have their handles tied together. And, of course, that having been done, it was exciting to knock at both doors then run up to the next landing from where we could watch opposing neighbours struggling to open their doors and pulling against each other in the process. Even without the handles tied, it was grand fun starting at a stairhead and running down, knocking every door on the way and escaping into freedom at the end of the close before being caught. I had the advantage of being very quick on my feet.

Life was not all spent on the street, there was school too. Like all the Roman Catholic girls in the neighbourhood (and most were) I attended St. Mungo's Convent School. And I remember my first day there vividly. 'I'll be here when you come out,' Mum reassured me as I left her. But that seemed forever away, at least it did until I met my teacher. Her name was Miss Bonny, and I thought she was beautiful. With black hair, long black eyelashes and a smile to gladden the heart of the most distraught five year old, she won me over. Miss Bonny gave me a square brown box with two things on it, my name and a gold star. It seemed to me that there was a whole world within that brown box, and all of it had to be discovered one little piece at a time. There were different coloured shapes of gummed paper, rods of plasticine and a pencil. And on top of them all was a sweet. 'Are these for me?' I asked. 'Yes,' Miss Bonny said, smiling. I'll never forget that smile. Nor have I forgotten my surprise that these things were for me and that they didn't need to be paid for.

Even on day one, school went downhill. Another teacher took my class for the second part of the morning, and she could not have been more different from Miss Bonny. 'Sit up straight,' she ordered. 'Fold your arms and look right ahead.' Squirming five year olds fixed themselves into position and an air of gloom descended on the classroom. Life seemed to have left the room with Miss Bonny. Regimentation had entered, a regimentation that was to characterise my days in St. Mungo's Convent School.

First thing each morning we said our prayers and recited the catechism. Long prayers and verbatim catechism answers worried me badly. Many evenings were spoiled fretting that I'd not remember my catechism answer and that my mind would go blank when I was asked for it. If that happened we were punished on the hand with a leather strap in front of the whole class, a humiliating experience. From time to time a priest visited the school, catechising us and questioning us on the different coloured vestments he wore on a Sunday, so checking on our chapel attendance.

Then there was the worst of all terrors, the confessional box, into which we went to confess our sins to the priest. Because we could not see the priest to whom we were confessing we always naturally assumed it was the most terrifying of the priests we knew. Sins were confessed, a routine round up of 'I've been cheeky to my mum. I don't like Mary in my class. I told a lie to my teacher and I didn't do what my dad told me.' But the real mortal sin was missing chapel. And that's what happened to me one Sunday. That week, when the teacher took us along for confessional, I waited in real fear of it being the priest I was most afraid of. And it was. I went through the usual preamble of childish sins then confessed to having missed chapel. There was a roar of anger. 'I've a good mind to send you to a protestant school as a punishment,' the disembodied voice bellowed.

It was a very distressed little girl who climbed the stairs home that afternoon. 'What's the matter?' Mum asked. Through my tears I explained what had happened. Mum, brought up a protestant but 'turned' on marriage to Dad, was furious. 'How dare he say that. I'll give him a piece of my mind!' she announced. 'And Maureen,' she added, 'if he ever says anything like that again, I'll take you away from St. Mungo's myself and send you to a protestant school. That wouldn't happen to you there.' I can still remember how proud I felt of Mum that day. She said she'd give the priest a bit of her mind and I knew she would.

Dad and Mum seldom went to chapel, but they made sure that we children did. Because we were not allowed to eat before the communion, our minds were firmly fixed on the state of our stomachs by the time we came towards the end of the 10 am mass. Despite the service being all in Latin we knew from the rituals when it was five minutes before the end and we were taken up with the prospect of bacon, egg, sausages, fried potato scones and tomato. The priest's final five minutes were lost on us as our minds went through the breakfast menu and our tummies rumbled in anticipation. Then there was the mile long sprint home, the dash up the stairs ... and the smell, the smell of bacon. Mum had it ready for us coming. Dad was nearly always in a good mood on Sundays and we enjoyed sitting down to this much looked forward to meal together. Those were precious family times. We listened to the big wooden box radio, to *Jimmy Clitheroe* and *Round the Horn*. Dad read the Sunday paper and John and I had our comics. Sundays were good days, at least they were after we got chapel over and done with.

Not everything about my Roman Catholic schooling was negative. There was Sister Mary Benedictine who was everything that my young mind imagined a saint would be. When she spoke about the Lord Jesus, her eyes lit up with love for him. And she loved us too. As a child I suffered often and badly from earache. I remember one morning when it was particularly painful, Sister Mary Benedictine stopped the class, brought me a hot drink and a biscuit and wrapped her own warm black fleecy scarf round my head, covering both ears. It was as though she wrapped me in her love and in the love of Jesus. That was when I decided that I wanted to be a nun. But what I gained from Sister Mary Benedictine was not a vocation, rather it was the beginnings of a realisation that faith in Jesus Christ was something real and personal, not rules regulations and rituals.

School, good or bad, only lasted for part of the day and nine months of the year. We had plenty of time to enjoy ourselves and we knew how to do it. The long summer holiday, for example, was the time for back court concerts. Some of the teenaged girls would decide on a date and on a back court then it was all action. A clothes line was commandeered, and sheets begged or borrowed. Net curtains were purloined as props and mothers' wardrobes searched for whatever was thought to be glamorous in McAslin Street. The younger children would be sent off to buy various colours of crepe paper at 6d a packet. Red and royal blue were favourites. Red had a particular value because if we licked it we could use it in place of lipstick for the girls and rouge for the boys!

The younger children were lined up and told what they had to do in the concert. Some sang, others danced, told a joke or did a magic trick. Because I had a good voice, I was always asked to sing. As the day wore towards concert time the audience began to gather. Mums sat on kitchen chairs in the back court, others hung over their window sills and encouraged us on. And, wonder of wonder, some dads and mums would join in too. When I was all dressed up and on stage, red crepe paper lipstick and all, singing my young heart out, I forgot I wanted to be a nun and knew that my place was on the stage. I'd be a grand singer. That's what I would be.

Even as a child I looked round our audiences and thought how wonderful it was that everyone could be happy together like that. I had been in many of the houses and I knew they were very poor. I'd seen husbands arrive back in various stages of intoxication on a Friday night, and I'd heard muffled screams from beaten wives and children. How I wished we could hold on to the magic of the back court concerts where the only tears that were shed were of laughter or emotion when a wee one did something especially sweet, and the laughter was long and loud.

McAslin Street and others like it were theatres, and not just for back court concerts. Everyone knew what happened in every other home. Tenement living did not lend itself to privacy. But the street was full of actors. Wives, who were regularly beaten and abused in all sorts of ways, patted powder puffs over their bruises, tied on their headscarves and faced the world with a courageous smile. Parents who misused their children called them affectionate names in public. And boys and girls, having seen and heard hard and hurtful things in their own homes, shut them away inside themselves as they closed the flat doors behind them, and skipped down the stairs.

No doubt we all had our own escape routes. From the hardness of what was around me, I know I had mine. My way of avoiding reality was to lie on my back and look up at the sky, at the blue expanse and the white wisps of cloud. My imagination allowed me to live in the clouds. The clouds were softness, yet a softness I could stand on. And there I could be close to God because I thought the baby Jesus lived up in the clouds. When life dealt its hard blows, I took myself to the softness of the clouds, for there was nothing hard there, nothing jagged, nothing sore, and from the midst of the soft cloudiness I could not even see the hardness from which I was escaping. Most of all, in my white soft cloudy world I could sing, I could sing into the great spaciousness of heaven.

For many of my friends the summer holidays

meant eight weeks off school and that was it. But every other year we actually went away on holiday! Most of Mum's family moved from Wales to the Midlands of England. My gran and grandad lived in Wigston Magna near Leicester. What excitement! We took the 9 am train from Glasgow's Central Station, having watched Mum making up loaves of sandwiches, egg and banana, and enjoyed the magic of the journey. Leaving the city behind us we rattled past fields of cows and sheep, we played guessing games, we speculated about who would be waiting for us, about what we would do in our holiday. And we ate the sandwiches, first of all the egg ones then, for pudding, the banana sandwiches, long ago turned an unappetising black but still tasting delicious. At first the miles sped past, but as we neared our destination the train seemed to slow down. How impatient we were to arrive.

But we did. And there to meet us was an aunt or uncle with, wonder of wonders, a car! 'This is the life I would love to have' I thought to myself. I felt at home in what I thought to be the luxury of it all! Eventually we arrived at Gran and Grandad's house and had the warmest of warm welcomes. My first stop was Grandad's back garden. It was made of the stuff Enid Blyton books were about. Grandad kept hens at the bottom of the garden and he allowed us to collect the eggs. You couldn't do that in McAslin Street!

My grandfather grew what seemed to be every

kind of vegetable. I was fascinated with the runner beans, loving to watch him making cane wigwams for them to grow up. Did they really all wind round the canes in one direction? But I think what interested me most of all was Gran's daily ritual. She would consider what she was going to cook then broach the subject with Grandad. 'I think we'll have marrow today,' she would say, and he would take us out to the garden to find just the right marrow in just the right state of readiness. 'We'll have swede today,' she would say sometimes, 'or cabbage.' And he was always able to pick what she needed. For a city kid, who knew that what you wanted was not always available at the local shop, to have it growing in your own garden was something very special.

But even holidays were not unadulterated happiness, especially if Grandad discovered that John and I had been up to mischief. Here the mortal sin was not missing chapel but stealing fruit from the neighbour's apple tree. For that heinous crime we could be shut in the dog shed for an hour. The dog, a lovely and kindly sheepdog, was not left there for company! I remember sitting outside the door of the dog shed reading a comic aloud to John so that he would not be too bored throughout his incarceration. It was a nice feeling being able to make things better for John, though doing that got me into some scrapes over the years! These were safe and happy times from which I never wanted to return.

2

Growing pains

'You can pray to Jesus anywhere,' one of the nuns at St. Mungo's Convent explained to the class, 'because he is everywhere.' I decided to test out the theory. Running to the girls' toilet block, I shut myself in one of the cubicles and spoke to Jesus. I was sure he heard me, so sure that I went back there often to speak to him. There was no formality in my prayers, just conversations with someone outside of myself, someone I visualised as being about my age, someone who would be my friend. I needed to talk, I needed a confidant with whom to share some deep things.

But my picture of Jesus didn't seem to fit in with what I was seeing and hearing around me.

'Please Sister,' I said to one of the less pleasant nuns.

The nun turned round. 'Yes?' she asked.

'Please Sister, when we go to confession, at the end of our act of contrition I say, "I will not sin again, amen."'

'Yes?' She wore a puzzled expression.

'But we do sin again, Sister,' I said. 'We always sin again. That's why we have to keep going back to confession.'

'Don't speak nonsense, child. Get on with your work.'

Having plucked up courage to ask my question, her dismissal left me like a deflated balloon. I was full of whys. Why do some nuns talk about a loving God when they are so hard? Why are some priests cruel? Why do they tell me do say what I can't do? I was afraid to tell lies. Why should I say I won't sin again when I know I will? Religion, when I applied my brain to it, seemed to produce more questions than answers. So, while I kept up my conversations with Jesus in the toilet block and went to chapel to dream about my bacon and egg breakfast, by and large religion went into the background of my young life.

'I'm not feeling well,' I moaned when I was wakened up one morning.

'What's wrong?' Mum asked.

'I don't know. I just don't feel well.'

'Is it your ears again? Have you got a sore ear?'

'No, it's not my ears,' I wiped away tears. 'I've got a sore head and I'm hot and I don't feel well.'

But I was to feel a lot less well before I felt any better. I was soon so ill that the doctor's help was sought. Pneumonia was diagnosed and I was off school for quite a long time and lost the beginning of primary six.

'So you're condescending to join us again,' my new teacher said sarcastically on my return.

I nodded.

Well, don't just stand there. Go to your seat and get your books out.'

A little while later I was aware that the class kept glancing from me to the teacher. I looked at her. Her face registered severe displeasure.

'You seem to be back in body but not in mind, Maureen,' the teacher snapped.

Wondering what she was talking about, I turned to my neighbour for enlightenment. 'She spoke to you but you didn't answer,' she whispered.

'Please miss,' I stammered. 'I didn't hear you.'

'Didn't hear!' she spat out. 'What you mean is that you didn't listen. You are off for weeks then you come back and don't listen to what I say. You'll have to do better than that, Maureen McKenna!'

From that day on I studied my teacher's lips when she spoke. Perhaps that was why she didn't like me, she may have thought I was avoiding eye contact with her. I wasn't, instead I was struggling to follow what she said.

'Take out your dictation jotters,' was the worst thing the teacher could say. As she dictated she moved about the room, turning her head in ways that meant I could not see her lips moving, and we couldn't ask her to repeat herself.

'Maureen McKenna, come out to the front,' was heard more and more often, and each time it heralded the strap.

My time under that teacher was lonely and frightening.

The following year my deafness was diagnosed

and a little more understanding came my way. As a result, I did much better in my final year at primary and had hopes of going to the senior secondary school. That was the school of my parents' choice too despite the fact that it meant the expense of buying a uniform. Many families could not afford that. My friend Ruth was in that situation. She came from a big family and, although she was a gifted girl, her parents could not even consider the expense of senior secondary education. That was my one crumb of comfort when I was told I would go to the junior secondary school. But what a culture shock! From a girls' only convent school we went to St. Rock's, a mixed junior secondary with over a thousand pupils. Thankfully Ruth and I were in the same class.

The pair of us never ran out of things to talk about. But one day in particular I nearly rendered her speechless.

'Wait till I tell you what happened yesterday,' I said when I met her at the school gate.

'Go on then,' she encouraged, 'tell me.'

I took a big breath. This needed savouring.

'Jean and I were going past Mrs. Jones's window,' I began, 'Mrs. Jones who lives next door to us.'

Ruth nodded in anticipation.

'Tom was hanging out the window when we passed. "Come and see this," he said to us. So we went and looked in his kitchen window. "Do you know what that is?" Tom asked us.'

'What was it?' Ruth asked excitedly.

'I'm just going to tell you.' I paused for a minute. Her interruption had broken the thread of my story. 'Well,' I continued, 'on the far wall next the bed recess there was a metal shiny kind of cupboard, about this high (I indicated 3 feet into the air) and square.'

My friends eyes were shining. She was a wonderful audience.

'And there was a door in the front of it...'

'A door!'

'"Do you know what that is?" Tom asked us. 'I said I didn't know and asked what it was. "That's a refrigerator!" he said. "A refrigerator!" said I. "A refrigerator that keeps things cold?" I asked. Tom said that was right.'

Ruth was nearly jumping with excitement. 'What happened then?' she asked.

'Tom opened the door, and there was milk in it, and butter and eggs.' I was really in the business of enjoying this.

'Eggs!' said Ruth. 'Eggs in a refrigerator in McAslin Street.'

I nodded my head till it nearly fell off.

'And what happened then?' she asked.

I'd saved this bit up. 'Tom opened a secret door inside the refrigerator and took out a wee square tray. "Do you know what that is?" he asked. I didn't. "That's ice," Tom told us. '"Ice?" I said. "And here's how you get it out," Tom said. He took it over to the sink and bashed it off the side of it. Wee squares of ice went everywhere!'

'What does he want ice for?' Ruth asked.

I admitted that I'd been wondering that myself.

'But there's something else,' I told my friend.

Her face was a picture. 'Something else besides the refrigerator?' she looked amazed.

'Tom opened the door to the lobby. "Do you know what that is?" he asked, pointing to a wee table in the hall. "Of course I know what that is," I said. "It's a telephone. I've seen them in the pictures."

'A telephone!! In McAslin Street!' Ruth was struggling for words. 'Did it work?'

I nodded. What satisfaction there was in telling a good story to an appreciative audience.

'When I'm grown up,' I confided in my friend, 'I'm going to have my own refrigerator and my own telephone.'

'And I'll have mine,' Ruth joined in. 'And we'll telephone each other and talk about the eggs in our refrigerators!'

Of such things were dreams made of. Reality was different.

'There's something I don't understand,' I said one night at tea time.

Dad looked up from his mince, potatoes and cabbage. 'There's a lot I don't understand either,' he said.

He saw my puzzled expression.

'I don't understand why you spend so much time playing games instead of doing school work, for one thing.'

'But they're not games,' I argued. 'They are sports. And Miss. Wolfe says if I work hard at sports I could have a future in them.'

'Miss. Wolfe! Miss. Wolfe! Are there no other teachers in St. Rock's School but Miss. Wolfe?'

I struggled, I really struggled to remember that when Dad raised his voice like this it was partly because he was deaf. For once I didn't argue any further.

'We had history today,' I announced the next night.

I caught the glimmer of a smile on Mum's face but turned away before it was reflected on mine. She knew exactly what I was up to.

'You can learn a lot from history,' Dad said. 'Book learning is what matters. That's what will get you out of McAslin Street.'

'I like McAslin Street,' my young brother Brian announced. He was four years old. I remembered back to when the street had been the centre of my world and was suddenly aware that I was growing up. My world no longer centred on home and on the street. I had begun to discover the world beyond. And, interesting though secondary school history was, it was the world of sport that beckoned. But I was learning other things than sport, I was learning how to humour Dad.

'You're looking pleased with yourself,' Mum smiled as I rushed in from school some days later and threw down my bag.

'Guess what?' I asked.

'You got all your sums right?' she questioned.

'Mum!' And that was said in the tone that will be familiar to every parent of a teenager. It is something between exasperation and sorrow that the poor parent is so lacking in understanding.

'What is it then?' Mum asked.

'Ruth and I have both been picked for the netball team!' I announced. 'And our first match is next week. Miss. Wolfe said it again, Mum.'

'Said what?' she asked.

'She said I really could have a future in sports.'

In my excitement I hadn't heard Dad come in.

'Sit down, Maureen,' he instructed.

I did. And I looked down too.

'I thought you'd started to grow up. You've not been talking so much about playing all these games...'

My mind wandered. I thought of the times I'd enthused about history and English and maths (never Geography!) just to humour Dad.

'... just you listen to me,' he went on. 'You're getting to be a big girl and it won't be too long before you leave school and start work. And there are things you need to know about that. When a girl comes to me for a job in the shop, I don't ask her if she can score a goal at netball or if she can swim twenty lengths of Townhead Baths. I give her a long list of figures to total. And I give her a grocery order to make up. That's what you should be working towards. You're not going to make a living out of playing tennis.'

It was about that time that I started leading a double life. At home I talked about school work, the kind of school work Dad approved of. When we had religious education, thankfully not every day as in primary school, I told him what I had learned. He read the compositions I wrote, and checked the grammar on any I did at home. I explained my maths problems to him, and he went over them. Working with figures was never a problem for Dad, he was at it every day. But for all of my talk about school, the love of my life was sport. I excelled at netball and tennis, but best of all there was swimming. And I swam like a fish. Townhead Baths, a short sprint from home, cost 4d. But 4d didn't grow on trees. Mine was usually got together by taking a glass lemonade bottle back to the shop for 3d and a 1d from Mum for doing an odd job, usually taking rubbish down to the midden in the back court. Tennis outside of school was a different matter altogether. You needed money and contacts, and I had neither.

'It's a nice feeling to be swimming for the school,' I told my friend Ruth.

She nodded. 'I know what you mean,' she said. 'I like being in the netball team. You kind of feel you matter.'

'Special,' I added. 'It makes you feel special, special and important.'

'We're special,' Ruth sang.

'And important,' I replied, moving the melody up a tone.

'And we matter,' Ruth sang on.

'That's us!' I finished with a flourish.

We linked arms and headed for the girls' door. Playtime was nearly over and we didn't want to be late for Miss. Wolfe and PE.

'We're special and important,' we sang as we laced our way between our fellow pupils, 'and we matter. That's us!'

And if anyone raised an eyebrow as we passed, Ruth and I looked at each other and grinned.

'Maureen,' said Miss. Wolfe, 'wait behind after the class, please. I want a word with you.'

That would have sent my heart plummeting had it been said by some of my other teachers, but when my PE teacher said it, I filled with anticipation.

'You're swimming is coming along wonderfully well,' she enthused.

I beamed.

'And I think you are ready for a challenge. Do you?'

I nodded my head. I didn't dare speak. What kind of challenge? I wondered.

'I'd like you to go for trials with a view to swimming for the South West of Scotland Team.'

I swallowed hard. I couldn't trust myself to speak.

'Would you like to do that?' Miss. Wolfe asked.

Would I! Would I want my dreams to come true? Was this really happening to me?

'Yes, Miss,' I replied. 'Yes please, Miss.'

I suppose my feet were on the ground when I left the gym dressing room, but my head and my heart were soaring.

Where was Ruth? I needed to tell Ruth.

The place was different. The atmosphere was different. The tone was different. Was I really in the same world?

'Your hearing is not as good as it was last time I saw you, Maureen,' the ENT specialist told me. 'And you are not helping the situation.'

I hung my head. Was it my fault I was becoming deaf?

'There are some things you really must avoid, things that cause extra pressure on your ear drums.'

I wanted to clap my hands over my ears. Don't say it! I shouted inside myself. Don't say it!

'Things like flying could cause you a problem,' he went on.

I let myself relax a tiny bit. Flying? I wasn't exactly going to be doing that once a week.

Suddenly I was aware of his eyes, they were boring right through me.

'And swimming,' the doctor said. 'I know it means a lot to you, but if you want to have any useful hearing left you'll have to stay out the water.'

He had said it! He had said the words! My hearing was bad and becoming worse, but suddenly my head was full of noise. I was screaming inside myself.

'Do you hear me?' he asked, not unkindly.

I nodded.

But you'll not take away my big chance, I thought to myself. You can't rob me of this. I'll not tell anyone. Nobody will know. I'll swim and nobody will know.

It was just days till the trials, days till my dream would come true, days till everybody would be clapping for me, Maureen McKenna, schoolgirl champion, member of the West of Scotland Team. That was all just days away and this man was trying to take it from my grasp. No way, I decided, no way would he do that.

'Thanks, Mum,' I said, as I left the house on the night of the trials. 'Thanks for everything.'

I walked down the stairs to the street below. Had it not been for the ENT specialist I would have ran. I might have flown. Under my arm, wrapped in a towel, was my new swimsuit and cap. Mum had bought them specially. The light roll of towel and swim kit felt as though it weighed a ton. Gradually, as I went in the direction of the trials, my steps slowed down. My spirit sank. I felt sick, sick at heart. And I couldn't even cry. Then I realised I had stopped. Turning round on that pavement was the hardest thing I had ever done. With each step of the way back, with each tread of the stairs, I aged. I was no longer a child when I pushed the door open.

'Are you all right,' Mum asked anxiously.

'No.'

'What's the matter?'

'I can't swim.'

She looked at me. I've no idea what went through her mind.

'The doctor says I'll get deaf if I swim again.'

There was real sorrow in Mum's eyes, sorrow and hurt and grown up things I couldn't have recognised before that night.

I heard my voice rising. 'Why do I never get to be the winner?'

Mum had no answer.

'I hate it!'' I shouted. 'It's just not fair!'

And I could see for a brief moment that Mum hated the unfairness of it too. But even she could not begin to dredge the terrible depths of my sorrow.

Dad did his best.

'There was never any future for you in swimming,' he said.

I sat, silent and sullen.

'You're a bright lassie. Now you can't swim you'll have more time for your school work.'

He was trying his best, but his best fell dismally short of the support I needed.

'And you'll get a good job when you leave school.'

He met a stone wall in response.

Unable to cope with the silence, he went on. 'Swimming was just a sport. You've got your whole life in front of you.' he finished weakly.

I snapped.

'It isn't just a sport for me! It is my life!'

Dad looked shocked at the rawness of my anger.

'Swimming means the whole world to me!' I ranted on. 'I hate it! I hate everything! I hate you!'

On any other occasion I would have had my hide tanned.

But I didn't.

Ruth understood.

Having nothing better to do with myself, I got down to some school work.

'There's a distinct improvement in the standard of your work,' my English teacher said half way through my third year at school. 'They were late in showing themselves, but there seems to be some brain cells there after all. Maybe they've come out of the dust in time,' she went on thoughtfully.

In time for what, I wondered. Some weeks later I found out.

'There's a letter for you to take to your parents,' the headmaster told me one day.

I knew I hadn't done anything he'd need to write home about, but I still felt guilty. Seeing my expression, he went on, 'You're a lucky girl, Maureen. If your parents agree to it, you're to be given the opportunity to go on to St. Gerard's Senior Secondary School.'

My head was all of a whirl. St. Gerard's? Me? Mum went up to the school, discussed it with the headmaster, and before I had got my head round the thought of it, I was told that I'd been accepted. Dad's contribution to the proceedings was to indicate he was proud of me, in a morose kind of a way.

Going on to St. Gerard's set me up as different. While my friends were out in the adult world finding jobs for themselves, I was putting on my school uniform and continuing my studies. I was also very short of money. Gone were the days when a few runs up and down stairs to the midden and a dash to the shops with two empty lemonade bottles was able to finance my needs. Something had to be done.

'Maureen McKenna,' a neighbour shouted out of her window to me, 'would you like a wee job?'

'What kind of a job?' I asked.

'I would give you two shillings if you would clean my stairs every Friday night.'

Two shillings! That was eight empty lemonade bottles! The decision was not hard to make.

'Yes, Mrs. Taylor,' I answered. 'I'd like to clean your stairs for you.'

'You'd have to do them well, mind,' Mrs. Taylor concluded.

'I will,' I promised. 'I'll make them shine.'

And I did.

Within just a few weeks I had five customers in all, extending over two closes and three stairs. I was in my element.

On Fridays I rushed home from St. Gerard's, went to Muirheads the grocery shop next door for a supply of tablets of whitewash (2d each), then dashed upstairs to get ready for work. Wearing one of Mum's pinnies and a pair of wellington boots, I emerged a little while later, bucket in hand. It may not seem exciting to be washing other folk's stairs, but it was during those Friday nights that my dreams and aspirations were all worked out. If I could make a difference to a close and stairs, I, Maureen McKenna, could make a difference to the world.

I started at the bottom, cleaning the close mouth before working my way up the stairs. As I progressed to the first landing, neighbours would come out to the sound of my singing. I always sang as I worked. 'Let's hear *Walking back to happiness*, Maureen,' old Mrs. Taylor said nearly every week. 'What about *As long as he needs me*,' another would suggest when I'd stopped singing. 'You know, the song Shirley Bassey sings,' she added. Of course I knew it, I knew all her songs and all Helen Shapiro's songs too. 'You'll be singing at the London Palladium, one day, young Maureen,' Mrs. Taylor would say. And I believed her.

The first landing done to my satisfaction, I turned the corner and headed up the second flight of stairs. What a grand feeling it was, starting off with the grime of a week's footfalls, and leaving it all whitewash white behind me. As I reached the top of each stairhead, it was less hard work as fewer feet climbed to these heights. At the top landing there was a huge skylight window, a window that made my work glow. One day, I thought, I'll climb a white stairway to the top of the world. That will be my heaven. Oh the satisfaction of standing at the top of four flights of sparkling stairs knowing it was all my own work. And the singing, there wasn't a stage in Glasgow with better acoustics than a tenement stairhead. But that wasn't all. For my evening's pleasure, and to me it was pure pleasure, I got twelve shillings to put into my Post Office book.

But life was not all sunshine and singing, as a visiting priest was to discover to his cost. Having been ignored for the duration of his visit, he turned to me before he left.

'God bless you,' he said, then added, 'God is good.'

'I don't believe that any more.'

He looked startled. 'Why?' he enquired.

'Because every time something good comes along in my life, just when I'm reaching out to take it, it is snatched away.'

'Have you prayed about it?' he asked.

'Prayed!' I barked. 'And what good has that ever done me? I'll never ask God for anything again because all he does is dangle things in front of me then yank them away.'

The priest opened his mouth to speak.

'I'd be a famous swimmer by now,' I told him, 'if God had answered prayer. I'd be somebody, not an overgrown schoolgirl dressed in a daft uniform when all my friends are out earning their living.'

'You're a wicked girl,' the priest announced.

'I'll be seeing you at confession.'

I was furious. 'No you will not! And you'll not be seeing me at chapel again either.'

'I think you should be quiet,' the priest said. 'You're a sinful girl and don't deserve it, but I'll pray for you.'

I'd gone so far that I couldn't stop. 'You'll be wasting your time,' I told him. 'I don't believe in your God any more. If I get anywhere in life it will be by my strength not his. And I will get somewhere, I promise. Just you wait and see, one day Maureen McKenna will be somebody!'

Despite knowing the opportunity that further education could bring, I just did not settle at St. Gerard's. After one year there, I left to work in my father's grocery shop.

'I hope you don't think you'll get any favours,' Dad told me before I started.

Having worked for him on Saturdays I already knew my place.

'You'll start at the bottom and work your way up like everyone else. And that means sweeping the floors and scattering the clean sawdust every day, washing the hen's muck off the trays of eggs, and being number eight behind the counter.'

My aspirations turned to desperation as I was faced with the most menial of jobs. It was years before I was able to say I was grateful for my father's training. At the time I hated it. And sometimes I even hated him.

But work had its compensations, it meant I had

a little money in my pocket and that I felt grown up. However, being grown up had its problems. I was an insecure and awkward teenager, especially where the opposite sex was concerned. Perhaps new clothes would give me confidence, I thought.

'Please, Mum, please let me have the money for some clothes. I look like a tramp beside the other girls.' That was always a good line with Mum. She took pride in her family's appearance.

After much persuading, Mum gave me enough to buy a dress that would accommodate a huge underskirt (how grateful we should be that such fashions don't last long!) and my first pair of stiletto heeled shoes. With my hair brushed up into a bouffant and held fast with lacquer (cement, Dad called it), I felt able to venture out and meet the world. But if Dad had seen me in full regalia I would never have made it through the door. That's why I left the house covered in a brown trench coat and wearing my old school shoes!

'Will we go to The Pally?' my friend Linda asked.

My heart thumped fit to burst through my rib cage.

'Yes, come on,' I urged.

There was general agreement among the group that The Pallais was where we would go, there to meet the loves of our lives. Having braced myself for the wonder of it all, what I met was utter humiliation.

'Is this always what happens?' I asked Linda in a whisper.

'Why, what's wrong?'

'What wrong! It's like a cattle market. Girls all lined up the side of the hall and boys swanking it up and down in front of them picking a partner like they'd pick a prize cow.'

I wanted to crawl back into my childhood, but there was no way back.

Having a job was not the answer to my insecurities. Growing up through my teens did nothing to increase my confidence. Finery didn't give me courage, so I looked for it in my friends. The more confident they were, the more secure I felt. I could hide in their confidence and pretend some of it was mine.

'What are you having to drink?' a friend asked one night.

I said the first thing that came into my mind. 'I'll have vodka.'

'On its own?'

'On its own,' I agreed. What company did it usually keep? I wondered.

But it parted company with me soon enough. It was just down, when it was up again. Oh, the mortification of it!

'Try it with orange juice,' someone suggested.

I did. At least it stayed down.

'I'll have another,' I said, beginning to enjoy the glow it gave me.

Little did I know that I had just made a friend, a friend that would one day try to destroy me.

I was eighteen years old.

3

A friend of a friend

'We've got so much in common,' I told my friend
Ruth.

She nodded.

'And I don't feel awkward with him,' I went
on. 'Most men make me feel like a fish out of water.
George is different.'

'Has he got a job?' Ruth asked.

'Yes, he works in a shop.'

'Well,' she said. 'You've got that in common.
What else?'

I thought before I answered. 'He comes from
the same kind of family as I do and was brought
up in the same kind of street.'

Ruth laughed heartily. 'You mean there's
another street in Glasgow like McAslin Street. I
don't believe it!'

'And we both like a good time,' I added.

Ruth agreed. 'So good you can't remember it
in the morning.'

But it was later when I was alone that I thought
Ruth's question through. What else did I have in
common with George? We had both had
knockbacks over the years and we were still sore
about them. But we'd reached the same conclusion,

when life kicked us, we'd kick back. We would work hard, make money enough to buy what we wanted as well as what we needed, and we'd both end up as somebodies. But would we do that better together or apart, that was the question I puzzled over. And I decided that we'd have more chance of winning if we were together. So George and I began a twelve year relationship. And when people showed disapproval, we laughed.

'You've made your bed,' Dad said, the day I left, 'and you can lie on it.'

Did he see that George had hidden depths?

Those were successful years and terrible years. As I give a brief account of them, I will relate no conversations. There are some things I don't want to remember.

Having decided to succeed, we worked hard, really hard. Most of the time we had our own businesses and they were successful until drink pulled the plug on them. When that happened, and it did several times, we dusted ourselves down and climbed out of the pit of our own making. And when we reached one of our goals, we made a higher one and aimed for it. The money rolled in, though we grafted for every penny. We earned enough to buy properties outright, then, when we'd bought the flat we'd set our sights on, we looked around for a better one. When we were driving the cars that appealed to us, we kept our eyes open for flashier models. To anyone looking on, we were the up and coming couple. We were becoming what we set out to be, we were becoming somebodies.

How tragically different things were inside our front door. George was an angry man. After our first two years together his anger became more than verbal, it exploded into violence. Although I had encountered violence in other circumstances, this was different because I was on the receiving end of it. A strange quirk occurs in the thought processes of those who are subjected to violence, a quirk that results in them thinking that somehow or other, in a way they can't fathom, they are responsible for what is happening to them. I worked harder and earned more to try to win George's favour. He hit me harder and all I did was earn more vicious assaults. I tried harder still, and he abused me in even more awful ways. Had his behaviour been just related to drink I could have understood it better. But it was not. It was plain viciousness. On one occasion I was so badly beaten that I ended up in hospital, ashamed and humiliated. It was weeks before I was fit for work again, and almost as long till I felt fit to be seen. It was my belief that George would kill me. So what did it matter if I drank myself insensible. At least I was then less aware of what was happening to me.

'Come in,' Mum said sadly, when I arrived at her door looking for refuge. By then Dad and Mum had moved from McAslin Street to a nice house in Knightswood, a house with a bathroom, much to their delight, and a garden all of their own.

Mum wiped tears from her eyes. 'Come in.'

'Don't cry, It'll be alright,' I assured her.

'But it's not alright,' she stifled a sob. 'Look at you, Maureen. You're black and blue.'

I couldn't trust myself to speak.

'Do you want a cup of tea?'

I shook my head.

'Away into your room, lass. Away and sleep it off.'

Mum will never know what it meant to me that she didn't invade my privacy, that she didn't pry into the situation that drove me so often to her door, that she just sent me to my room where, like a wounded animal, I curled up in the foetal position and hoped that I would die.

In my desperation I hurled abuse at God, accusing him of kicking me every time I was down. I didn't doubt that God was there, and in a strange way that was a comfort to me, but all I wanted to do was to shout at him, throw my hurt, my anger and my desperation in his direction. And, if I thought God wasn't listening, I raged at him for abandoning me.

Alcohol became my dearest friend. When I felt out of my depth, I took a drink. When I wanted to die, I drank to give me the courage to stay alive. For the truth was that I was as afraid of death as I was of life. With a few drinks inside me I could lose some of my cares and worries, finding relief in a plastic sort of way and in a make-believe world. I tried my childhood escape route, searching the clouds for comfort, but the clouds were hard. I assessed my situation. At 32 years of age I had a successful business, a nice home and a good car. But my life had no direction, no meaning and absolutely no hope.

On many occasions I tried to break free, to escape from the relationship that was killing me. But I discovered a terrible truth. When someone is caught in a cycle of violence and abuse of every kind, their abuser holds them in a web from which they can't escape. They are brainwashed into believing that they are to blame, that they are the cause of the violence and that if they go they take that problem with them so that nobody will want to know them. They have no route down which to escape. It becomes part of their mindset that they are in a prison of their own making, that the only way out is in. So they stay. And often the company they keep in their loneliness comes out of a bottle or through a syringe. I drank, and for all the good it did me I might as well have hit myself over the head with the bottles.

I am unable to say more, but those twelve years cast a long shadow.

'Have you ever played the glad game?' Mary asked.

'The what?'

'The glad game, sometimes called the Polyanna Experience.'

'No,' I told her. 'What is it?'

'When I was going through my roughest patches,' she explained, 'I'd think about glad things. Sometimes they would be nice things from when I was a girl, though there were few enough of them, or funny things from school, or what I used to get up to with my mates. It takes my mind off what's really happening in my world.'

I looked at Mary. She was older than me, but we'd been through so much in common that the age difference meant nothing at all.

'OK then,' I said. 'You start.'

Mary thought for a minute. 'I remember when I was a wee girl being sent to the grocer for a pennyworth of broken biscuits. Mum was always pleased with me because I never opened the bag before I got home. What she didn't know was that the old man in the grocer's shop had a soft spot for me and he always gave me a ha'penny humbug. That's why I always volunteered to go!'

We laughed at the thought.

'And I remember how we used to get all dressed up on the first Sunday of May every year. Weeks before that all the mums went to a wee dressmaker's shop in our street to put in orders for our dresses. They were always pink or blue gingham. It didn't matter that everyone was dressed the same on the big day, we all thought we were swells in our new dresses and our black patent buckled shoes and white bobby socks. I used to walk up and down McAslin Street all day looking at my reflection in my shoes!'

Mary and I giggled like girls.

'I don't believe this,' I said, when the giggles subsided. 'Here we are, a pair of alcoholics away for an AA Convention, and we're sitting in our bedroom playing the glad game.'

'But we're not drinking,' commented Mary.

'What's AA done for you?' I asked.

She sat quietly for a minute or two before answering. 'I think it has given me hope,' she said. 'I don't need to tell you what life with the old man was like, you've been through it yourself, but that kind of experience leaves you hopeless.'

I nodded in agreement. How right she was.

'But coming to AA helps me see that there maybe is hope, just maybe. But I'm not sure I'll make it. I'm struggling, Maureen,' she confided. 'I'm really struggling.'

I gave her a hug.

But Mary was a fighter. She gave herself a shake, quite literally, looked me in the eye and asked what AA had done for me.

'It's about hope as well,' I told her. 'There are folk here who've been through what we've been through and they've been dry for years now. I know they need to keep coming, but I wouldn't mind that if I thought I could get through life without refreshments.'

'Refreshments!' spat out Mary. 'That's a cruel word. There's nothing refreshing about the drink.'

I knew she was right, but somehow refreshments sounded less ugly that booze.

Mary, dear Mary, how I wish I could thank her for her acceptance and love. It saw me through some dismal days.

'How long have you been coming to AA?' the man who was serving tea and coffee at our dinner dance asked me.

He introduced himself as Hugh McKenna.

'Think we're related?' I laughed. 'I'm Maureen McKenna! I've been coming for two and a half years now.'

'And how are you coping?'

There was something striking about Hugh. There was real joy in his face and he had an ease and grace about him that I'd not met before.

'It's good not being dependent on drink,' I told him. 'But I'm not out of the woods yet. What about you? You look as though you're doing well.'

Hugh made himself comfortable beside me. 'The only reason I'm doing at all,' he said, 'is because I'm a Christian.'

Big deal, I thought, religion did nothing for me. Hugh read my response on my face.

'I was brought up a Catholic,' he said, 'but my life was just one mixed up mess. I kept looking for peace and when I didn't find it I drowned my disappointment in drink. Coming to AA gave me some kind of stability, but it was Christ who gave me peace.'

Hugh was so sympathetic that, when we next met, I poured out my heart to him, horrors and all.

'I've met somebody who could help you,' he told me, when I had finished my tale of woe. 'He's a real friend, someone I completely trust. He gave me what I most needed, he gave me back hope.

And he filled up all the empty spaces in my life, so much so that I don't need to keep on searching because I've found someone who can give me everything I need. He can do the same for you, Maureen.'

'Who is he?' I asked. 'Could I meet him?'

'Yes,' said Hugh. 'You could meet him. His name's Jesus.'

'You're kidding!' I laughed. But I didn't laugh for long. I could see peace in Hugh's face and seriousness.

'Jesus means everything to me,' he said earnestly. 'He's real and he's alive. I know because I've met him. Having real faith is nothing like the religion we were brought up with. It's not about priests and confessionals. It's not about keeping petty rules and regulations. Faith's a relationship,' he explained, 'a relationship with Jesus. He's alive, Maureen, and he wants to come into your life. All you need to do is ask him.'

I tried to take in what he was saying. Hugh saw I was struggling.

'Think about it. And if ever you want to know more about my friend, phone me.' He rose to go. 'I'll pray for you.'

I'd heard these words before, from the priest in McAslin Street. But I didn't tell Hugh that he'd be wasting his time.

What a comparison it was, to leave that lovely conversation, so full of hope and possibility, to go back to George. And he seemed to sense that I'd begun to find a way out, for he became more violent and abusive than ever. One night, after a particularly harrowing experience, I once more ended up at Mum's house bruised and broken. But there was something different. I remembered that Hugh was praying for me and that seemed to give me strength.

'God,' I said, tentatively. 'Can you hear me? I don't know how to speak to you. Can you just help me, please?'

Suddenly I knew with a certainty that the violence wasn't all my fault, that I wasn't to blame for all the abuse. I could leave George. His web didn't need to hold me forever. For over a week I kept mostly to my room in Mum's house, struggling to build up strength and courage for what I knew I needed to do.

'I'll look after you,' my brother Brian told me over and over again. 'I'll keep you till you can keep yourself. You need to do it,' Maureen,' he insisted. 'Or the only time you'll leave George is in a coffin.'

I shuddered at the truth of what he was saying.

'You can get another job in a different part of Glasgow,' Brian went on. 'You can turn your hand to anything. You could always drive a bus!'

I laughed with him till I cried.

Mum looked relieved to see tears of laughter rather than despair. She decided to keep the mood light.

'Go on, Maureen, tell us about the family bus driver. It's a good story.'

I sat back in the chair and smiled at the memory of my bus driving days.

'Come on,' Brian added, 'let's hear it.'

This is lovely, I thought, just being together and not being afraid.

'Well,' said I. 'Where will I begin?'

'The beginning,' came as a chorus.

'Right! You've asked for it. I'd always had an ambition to be a bus driver,' I started, 'I don't know why. So one day I went into Cumbernauld bus depot and asked how you trained to be a driver. One of the inspectors asked me why I wanted to drive a bus. I told him I just did. They organised a trial run around the town in a single decker and I still remember the exhilaration of getting behind this big wheel and steering the bus round corners. "There's a woman at the wheel!" someone shouted. I liked that too! So I was accepted for training along with three young men. You can imagine their comments. But all they said just made me more determined to get through the test. And I did! The instructor was delighted, I was the first woman he'd put through.'

'Go on,' Brian said. 'Tell us about Ernie.'

'And about your uniform,' added Mum.

I'd not enjoyed an evening like this for ages.

'Well, there was no uniform for women drivers because there were no women drivers to wear them. So I was allowed to buy my own. I chose a pretty pink checked blouse and a blue one to change with. These went well with smart black trousers. The only part of the uniform I wore was the light cotton summer jacket. But the drivers were none too pleased when I arrived for work so well turned out.'

Brian was sitting waiting for Ernie. So I decided to oblige.

'One day I had to go into Glasgow's Buchanan Street Bus Station, My conductor, Ernie, who was six feet tall and nearly as broad, was always game for a laugh. I arrived at the dock to take the 5.30pm run to Cumbernauld. The bus was a 'full swinger', bus driver slang for jam-packed.

"Will you help me play a joke on the passengers?" Ernie asked me.

"Like what?"

"Like you putting on my conductor's ticket machine and money pouch and letting me have your driver's badge. I'll get up behind the wheel and you start collecting the fares. We'll swop over before time, but let's play it for a laugh."

I didn't need any persuading. We swopped gear and I started doing the conductor's job.

"Maureen" his voice came from the cab.

"What?"

"I'm fed up driving this bus. Would you give me a break? I'll take the fares for you."

"But what'll I do?" I asked.

"You come up here and I'll show you. Just do this one run. I need a break."

Ernie climbed down from the cab, put on his money pouch and ticket machine and handed me the driver's badge. I hoisted myself into the cab and sat behind the wheel. The comments were priceless.

"You're not going to let a woman drive the bus!"

"I'm getting off if she's driving."

"Will you not just give me a chance?" I begged, struggling to contain my laughter.

Ernie tried to reassure them. "She'll do just fine." They were not reassured.

Just then the inspector came up.

"You're two minutes late in leaving," I was told.

I turned on the engine, got into gear and released the handbrake, but not before I had looked in the mirror. The expressions were priceless, and some passengers were even knocking on the window to draw the inspector's attention. Leaving the bus station, I approached the worst corner in Glasgow, one that was especially bad with a full load of passengers and they knew it. I eased the bus round the corner, straightened her up and felt a sigh of relief behind me. Only then did Ernie admit to the folk on board that I was actually the driver and that he was the real conductor!'

Mum laughed. It was so good to see her laughing, she'd been through such sorrow with me.

'Funny that,' she said. 'You being a bus driver.'

Yes, I thought. Very strange.

A few days later, I decided to go back to the flat I had shared with George to collect some things. It would be my last contact with him. I knew I had to make the break now or be broken. Over the week at Mum's I had prayed a lot and pleaded with God to give me strength to do what I had to do. I asked Brian to give me a run.

'Where are you going?' he said, when he heard where I wanted dropped.

I told him.

'Please, Maureen, please don't go back there. You don't need to get anything. I'll buy you all you need.'

But I'd made up my mind. I got out of the car and walked along the road, it was my intention to get money at a cash machine then go to the flat. As I walked, I looked at the people I was passing, couples talking, children skipping and laughing, women carrying baskets of shopping. How normal everything looked, I thought. If only I could have been one of these normal people. Suddenly I reached the lowest point of my life. I had never, even at the worst times, reached this black hole before. I could not face any more. I'd had all I could take.

I realised I was crying, walking and crying. My vision blurred. I couldn't see where I was going. Taking myself to the edge of the pavement, I stood there, rubbing the tears from my eyes, blinking to clear my vision. I was looking for a bus, any bus. It didn't matter what bus came, any one would do. One appeared in the distance. I stood there, utterly alone and in deep despair, bracing to throw myself under its wheels. 'God! I screamed inside myself as the bus came nearer. 'God help me!' A hand touched my shoulder, warmth seemed to flow from it, up to my head and down through my body. A calm swept over me. I turned round to see who was holding me. There was nobody there, nobody I could see. The bus was stopped now, at the bus stop along the road. People were getting on and off, and I was still on the kerb, I was still alive.

'Hugh McKenna speaking,' the voice said at the end of the phone.

'It's Maureen,' I said, 'Maureen McKenna.'

'I'm glad you phoned. I've been praying for you.'

'I've got to talk to you, Hugh, I've just tried to throw myself under a bus, but a hand on my shoulder stopped me and when I turned round there was nobody there.'

'Where are you?' he said urgently. 'And I'll come right away.'

'I'm alright,' I told him. And the calmness of my voice must have reassured him.

'Are you sure?'

'Sure. I'm going to the flat to collect some things then I'm heading back to Mum's. I've decided to break with George once and for all.' I heard my voice and was amazed at my confidence.

'Will George be there?'

'No,' I told him. 'He's at work. I'll be alright.'

'Give me your Mum's address,' Hugh said. 'And I'll come and see you this evening.'

I gave it to him.

'See you later.'

'I'd like that ... and thanks.'

I rung off.

It felt so strange going into the flat knowing it was the last time I'd be there. Having gone to collect my things, I discovered that nothing there was important to me. There was a crucifix on the wall. Kneeling in front of it, I asked Jesus to come into my life and to take control of it. Suddenly my former life welled up inside me and I asked him to forgive me. 'I don't really understand how it works,' I told God, 'but please, please help me make a break with my past and help me to make a fresh start.' There were no blinding lights, no voices from heaven, just an immense peace, a feeling of love and warmth and confidence, and of freedom from fear. Hugh was right, I realised, Jesus is alive! He had to be. I could feel his love alive inside me and around me. The warmth I was feeling was the warmth of personal love. Nothing, but nothing, could have been more different from religion as I had known it. Taking only a small bag containing some letters and a couple of photographs, I left the house, I left George and I left my past behind me.

4

New beginnings

'I've prayed for this day for years,' Mum said, when I told her I'd left George once and for all. 'And I'll stick by you.' She smiled at me. 'You look better already,' she added, a little wonderingly.

I didn't try to explain what had happened. I didn't really know what had happened.

'Is Maureen here?' Brian shouted urgently as he came in from work later that day.

'I'm here.'

'Thank heavens!' he breathed. 'I've been worried out of my mind. I take it George wasn't there.'

'I knew he wouldn't be.'

'Did you get your things?'

'Nothing mattered,' I told my brother. 'I decided not to take anything.'

Brian looked up.

'Dad would have been glad to know you've broken with George,' said Mum.

I agreed. But Dad had died a year and a half before.

Tea time that night was a mixture of Brian's offers to do anything he could to help me and relieved silences.

'Who's that at the door?' Mum asked anxiously, when the doorbell rang later that evening. 'Could it be George?'

'I think it's Hugh McKenna,' I told them.

Brian and Mum looked puzzled. Hugh McKenna? Who was he for a McKenna?

'Thanks a lot for coming,' I smiled at Hugh, holding the door wide open for him to come in.

I introduced him to the family and we settled into a relaxed conversation. But it was a conversation such as the McKenna household had never known before. Hugh talked about his faith naturally and without even a hint of preaching. He didn't come across as 'religious' at all, even when he took out his Bible to show me what it said.

'I'm beginning to understand,' I admitted, 'but there's so much to take in.'

'That's how it should be,' Hugh laughed. 'If we could take in all God is and does we'd be greater than God himself!'

'Right enough,' I agreed.

'But don't worry, God has reached down and held you when you were at your lowest ebb. That's where to start from. Other things will come with time. By the way,' he asked. 'Do you go to church at all?'

I shook my head, but I resolved to do something about that. Hugh didn't push the issue.

'What did you think of Hugh?' I asked Brian later, when my friend was safely on his way home.

My brother considered the question. 'He's nice,

and seems very sincere. He's not your regular kind of religious guy.'

'I've met men like him before,' Mum said, 'down in Wales when I was a girl. There were men there like Hugh. They never stopped talking about God. They were good men though, always there when they were needed.'

My life had turned on its head. Just a few weeks before, I'd had a home, a job, money in the bank, and I was without hope and without God. Now I was alone, homeless, penniless, happy and safe. And to my utter amazement and delight, I knew God loved me and I was beginning to fall in love with him.

On the first Sunday after I met with the Lord I set out to go to chapel. When I arrived at the door of the chapel, I looked across the road - right into a small church's open door. I'd never even noticed it existed before. Crossing the road, I made my way to what I discovered was a Baptist church. I had not been in a Baptist church before, and I wasn't sure what to expect. Uncertainty embarrassed me, as did the welcoming smiles of those who looked up when I went in. I sat in the first empty seat I could find and slid as far along as I could. It was November. There was a radiator at the inside end of the pew, and I found myself almost sitting on top of it. If I was red with embarrassment when I sat down, it was not long before I was bright red with heatstroke!

'Hello,' said a young woman who sat down

beside me. 'I'm Elizabeth McCormack. Is this your first time here?'

'I'm Maureen McKenna,' I replied. 'And I've not been before.'

I could have hugged her for not asking any more about me.

In came the minister. Picking up a guitar, he began to lead the lively and joyful worship. To say that this was different from what I had expected would not begin to describe the truth. I was gob-smacked! Were these folk really as joyful as they seemed to be? Or was this all some kind of religious hype? It sounded sincere enough.

'I want to talk about some words in Joshua chapter 24,' the minister, Dean Buchanan, announced. Everyone flicked to the page in their Bibles. I picked up mine and thumbed around it, not having the first clue who Joshua was or where to find him. Elizabeth came to my aid.

Dean read the words. 'Choose for yourself this day whom you will serve ... but as for me and my household, we will serve the Lord' (v 15). My mind wandered. What if anyone from St. Ninian's had seen me come into the Baptist church? Would God be angry with me for not going to the chapel? Suddenly Dean's words shot through me, and he seemed to boom out the words, 'Choose for yourself this day whom you will serve'. And I knew that was God's word for me. From then on I was riveted, listening to every word. For the first time in my life I was sorry when a sermon ended. Dean went to the door at the close of the service. Hiding among those who were leaving, I hoped to get away unnoticed. But a hand slipped though the worshippers and grasped mine.

'Welcome,' the minister said. 'I hope you enjoyed the service.'

'Yes thanks.'

'You're new here, aren't you?'

I nodded.

'Do you live locally?' he asked.

I gave him Mum's address.

'Would you like me to visit you?'

I panicked! What would Mum say? What would the neighbours think? Baptist ministers just didn't go to Catholic houses!

I told him what my background was, then agreed to a visit. A week later, I didn't know which was funniest, watching Dean's face or Mum's and Brian's. Thankfully the minister was sensitive to the situation, and they were too!

The following Sunday I was in no doubt about which church I should go to, though I did cross the road before I was right at the door of St. Ninian's! That day I met Anne Kelly, who welcomed me to the church and invited me to her home and into her heart. When I went to see her soon afterwards, we shared coffee and biscuits and life. Anne allowed me to talk and be silent, to laugh and cry. Dean and his wife Anne and Anne Kelly supported me throughout the next year of discovery. Most discoveries were positive, but some were not, like the morning I discovered George waiting for me as I left church. That day I discovered boldness in a relationship that had been marked by cowering fear.

'Everything is over between you and me,' I told him firmly. 'There is no place now in my life for violence and abuse. I'm not allowing you to hurt me any more.'

His face contorted as I spoke.

'My life has started all over again and you have no part in it,' I went on. 'I've now got a friend called Jesus and he'll protect me.'

George looked at me through steely eyes, then turned round, got into his car, slammed the door and drove away.

Life developed a pattern, especially after I found a job as a motor parts delivery driver. My days were spent happily driving about the city, delivering parts to a long list of garages. Never before had I known what real happiness was and, from some of the comments I got from mechanics, my state of mind was reflected on my face. Occasionally I was able to talk to the men about my Lord. If God opened doors of opportunity, I usually went through them.

I didn't see Hugh for some time because I stopped going to AA meetings, I felt no need of them. The Lord had completely taken away my desire for drink. Hugh phoned from time to time.

A year or so after I was converted, the phone rang. It was him.

'Hello,' he said. 'I was wondering if you'd like to go out for a run and a cup of tea.'

'I'd love to,' I replied, stifling the excitement I felt.

We made an arrangement to meet. The day dawned gloriously sunny, and we set off for Loch Lomond.

'Isn't God wonderful,' Hugh said, when we stopped in Glen Douglas to admire the view, 'he made every bit of this.'

I agreed, and thought to myself what a fine man this was beside me. That was the first of many runs, and the beginning of my love for Hugh McKenna.

As I got to know him better, I was struck over and over again by his steadfastness. Hugh refused to compromise, searching in the Bible for what was right and wrong, and sticking to what he found there. When I argued about things with him, he never got flustered. He just took out his Bible and showed me why he believed what he did. But there was nothing bullying in his approach, rather he was a gentle and kindly mentor.

'I hope you know what you're doing,' Mum said one day. 'I don't want to see you hurt again.'

'This is different, Mum,' I assured her. 'Hugh's not like George. Hugh's a Christian and a gentleman.'

'So he seems,' my mother conceded. 'But before you moved in with George nobody ever thought he'd nearly murder you.'

Brian decided to intervene. 'That's enough,

Mum. She knows what she's doing. And Hugh's different altogether.'

I knew that was true, but was I wise to let myself fall in love? I wondered.

Hugh was patient and sensitive over our two year long courtship. By the time he asked me to marry him, there were no doubts in my mind. I loved him deeply and had discovered that Hugh was the same through and through. The months before we were married held their trials. I believe the devil was trying to break us apart because he knew that God had work for us to do. But in God's battle with the devil, Satan is always the loser. We were married on 1st June 1984 in St. George's Tron Church in Glasgow, the congregation of which Hugh was a member. His minister, Rev Eric Alexander, married us. By then Mum had come to love Hugh too. His parents welcomed me into their family. Life was good.

Later that day we set off for two weeks honeymoon in a borrowed caravan in Arbroath, but somewhere along the way we took a wrong turning or two and found ourselves fifty miles from where we ought to have been.

'I'm gonna tell ma mammy oan you,' I said in my best Glasgow accent.

Hugh laughed. 'Did A no' tell ye, ye don't staund a chance wi' me. A canna even fin' ma way hame!'

I'd never had a relationship that allowed for that kind of banter. And in the two weeks we spent at

Arbroath, I felt that God had made up for all my years of trauma. I felt so respected, loved and cherished by the man I had married. Each morning Hugh read a passage from Scripture and we talked about what it was saying to us then prayed it through together. Since the first day of our married life, that has been central to our relationship.

In the caravan next door to ours was a family with ten year old twin boys. Before we'd been there a day, they discovered that Hugh was a very good footballer. (He still thinks that some big football club missed its chance by not signing him!) From then on there was a knock on our door each morning.

'Is Hugh coming out to play?' asked either Joseph or Matthew.

Then a voice from the door of their caravan. 'Leave them be! They're on their honeymoon!'

What did that matter to two little boys? They wanted their playmate.

Hugh, dressed in tee shirt and shorts, spent hours kicking their ball around with them.

He'd make a good dad, I thought, but that's not for us. Never in my time with George had I yearned to have children. Thank God for that. A child was a complication I certainly did not need then. Babies, I thought, were for other people, not for me. And such was the extent of the abuse I had endured that there was no likelihood I would have one.

After two wonderful weeks, we went home to our little house in Summerston. It was really just a modern room and kitchen with a bathroom, but a bit more upmarket. We were proud of it. I was even proud of having a mortgage! Previously, George and I had bought houses outright. There was no question of us doing that. We hardly had enough for the deposit. Hugh's job with The Talbot Association was not well paid but it was worthwhile and he really loved it. His work was with men in need, many of them with drink problems. This involved shift work. My part time shop job helped eke out our income.

Within a couple of weeks of returning home from Arbroath, I began to feel unwell. I'd had health problems in the past, and was concerned about what was wrong. Although he knew I was off-colour, I played down my worries to Hugh. I didn't want to upset him.

'You're looking a bit rough,' June, my sister-in-law, told me one day when she was in for coffee. 'Are you feeling alright?'

I admitted I wasn't.

'What's wrong?' she asked.

I described my symptoms.

'You should go and have a pregnancy test,' she announced.

I laughed.

'The chances of me ever having a baby are almost exactly nil!'

Although the thought stayed in my mind, I didn't mention it to Hugh. I should have done, he was beginning to be as worried as I was about what might be wrong with me.

Two weeks later June was back.

'You're definitely pregnant!' she announced, as she came in the door, and she would not let the subject go.

'Make an appointment with the doctor right away,' she ordered at the end of her short stay.

June is one determined lady! I took her advice and saw my GP two days later.

'It's really very unlikely,' my doctor said kindly. 'With your history I think we'd be wise to run some tests to find out what's causing the symptoms. But would you like me to do a pregnancy test just in case?'

I said I would.

'Please don't build your hopes up,' she cautioned before I left. 'Phone in three or four days for the result and we'll take it from there.'

The days before the result came back were lost in a haze of baby thoughts. Was it possible, just possible I was expecting? Wasn't I too old? I was 37. With my history, could I carry a baby? Could that really happen? Could we become parents? Where was Mothercare anyway ... you can't think about having a baby and not think of Mothercare? But the money! We'd committed ourselves to a mortgage and I'd have to give up my job. Then I thought about Joseph and Matthew in Arbroath. Hugh had been so good with them. How he'd love a son. My mind was a jigsaw of pieces, every one of them about babies, and I couldn't fit any of them together. We prayed, how we prayed.

72

I struggled to take in what the doctor was saying on the phone.

'Please try not to be too disappointed.' Her tone was very kindly. 'I'm so sorry.' There was a silence.

'Are you sure it's negative,' I asked, voice wavering.

'Quite sure,' she insisted. 'I'm sorry. If the symptoms don't go away in the next few days make another appointment to see me. We'll really need to have them investigated.'

I plummeted. If I'm not pregnant, I decided, I'm dying. After years of wanting to die, I now want to live ... and I think I'm dying. My imagination took me down many medical corridors, some I'd been wheeled along before and others I'd only heard of.

'So that's that,' I concluded, having poured out the doctor's news and my concerns to my husband of just a few weeks.

He put his arms round me tenderly. 'You're so precious to me,' he whispered, 'but you are even more precious to the Lord who knows all things. Let's pray about it.'

'Hugh ...' I said, 'will you pray that this new longing for a child will go away if it's not God's will we should have one. Pray that I'll get back to where I was before and feel that life is complete without a baby. Just now I feel empty.'

And that's what he prayed.

June arrived again some days later, and was

even more insistent that I was expecting a baby. My symptoms were alarming. If I had been pregnant I would have thought I was going to miscarry. June was clearly worried when I explained what the doctor had said.

'You've got to have another test done,' she stated.

There was no room for argument. The following day Hugh took a test to a private clinic in town. I lay in bed watching the tiny television he had put into the bedroom for me. Suddenly I caught the words, 'And Sarah laughed'. The programme was about the birth of Abraham and Sarah's son, Isaac. I had become aware of what was on at the point in the story where the elderly Sarah laughed at the news she was pregnant. God spoke to me through that programme. Suddenly, like Sarah, I was laughing. So although it was not a surprise to me when Hugh came home with a positive result, it was a tremendous delight. There were no words to describe our joy. However, in the light of the test result, my symptoms were alarming. Hugh phoned the doctor and I was rushed to Glasgow's Stobhill Hospital.

For several days I was in a kind of limbo. My symptoms persisted, the radiologist could not find a foetal heartbeat, not even a flicker of life, and I was on total bedrest. The staff was wonderful, tender and supportive. Despite the situation I had a kind of peace, knowing that God's will would be done and that his will was always for the best. Hugh spent many hours by my bedside, praying for me and for our unborn child. Then, when the wonderful day came when the scan revealed a heartbeat, I was scared to react in case the movement would damage our child. When I phoned Hugh with the news, I was only able to say a word of two before we both dissolved in tears, tears of sheer relief and thankfulness.

That was the beginning of what seemed a very lengthy pregnancy as I had to remain in hospital till I reached term. The months passed so slowly, but eventually the end of the year drew near. On Christmas Eve I was the only patient in the ward. As a special dispensation Hugh was allowed to stay with me beyond visiting time, but by 10pm I was so tired that I asked him to leave. Lying back in the stillness and darkness of my small world, feeling the baby kicking inside me, I suddenly started to cry. I think I cried for all the hurts that were trapped inside me, just as trapped as my unborn baby. And I wept for the world's sorrows too, for the babies aborted in the time I'd been in hospital and for the women I'd seen coming in full of hope and leaving empty-handed. I cried for children all over the world who, at Christmas, would be hungry, homeless, hurt, abused. I wept all my hurts and all my sorrows to the Lord. And I know he heard me and I know he cared.

At midnight two nurses came into the ward with gifts for me.

'Merry Christmas,' one of them said.

'We're saying a wee prayer for you,' added the other.

That meant so much.

When I was eight months pregnant I was allowed out for a visit to Mothercare!

On 12th March, at 1.50pm our darling son Paul was born. The child I thought I would never have lay cradled in my arms. We laughed and we wept and we prayed. And God understood.

5

Night feeds to night patrol

While loving my new born baby was a thrill and a delight, the practicalities of motherhood did not come naturally to me. I suppose, having been so long in hospital and so short a time married before that, I was really getting used to being newly married, having our own little home and being a first time mother all at once. Hugh worked shifts at The Talbot Centre which meant my routine, such as it was, varied from day to day. By the time Paul was six or seven months old, I had just about got things together. That was when Hugh came home with some news.

'I think it's time I left The Talbot,' he said one evening.

Because I knew Hugh loved his work I knew this was serious.

'The shifts don't make life easy for you,' he explained, 'and depending on what shift I'm working I sometimes don't see Paul awake for days at a time.'

That had certainly been true.

Hugh went on. 'And I believe God is calling me into full-time Christian service.'

We had talked about this a lot. His work with alcoholics was fulfilling in its own way, but Hugh knew that the answer to their needs was not only social care, but the good news of Jesus Christ. Other areas of work would allow for more open sharing of the gospel.

'You know I'm right behind you,' I assured him. 'But what kind of thing could you do?'

Hugh opened his newspaper, pointed to an advertisement, and handed it to me. Glasgow City Mission was advertising for night patrol workers.

That was a long evening. We discussed the job, so far as we understood it. We considered the drop in salary and our need to pay the mortgage, the constant nightshift and Paul being able to see his daddy during the day. We discussed it from every angle but kept coming back to the same point. If God was calling Hugh to be a Glasgow City Missionary, there was no way either of us would want him to do anything else. We laid out all the facts before the Lord in prayer and ended the evening by deciding that Hugh should apply for the job. If it wasn't God's will for him to get it, we believed that he wouldn't be accepted. He was.

On Thursday 6th March, 1986, Hugh did his first night patrol. His work involved going by van into the city centre at night with a stock of soup, bread and sandwiches. Having parked the van and loaded himself up with food, he sought out people in need of help or sleeping rough. He very soon got to know where the skippers were. Skippers are places where homeless folk congregate at night and they can be in the most bizarre places. Sometimes he came across dangerous situations, particularly in the bowels of the buildings in Glasgow's Anderson district, where fights would break out over the smallest thing. Before he went out to work, we prayed together for the people he would meet, and for Hugh's safety throughout his patrol. He says he never felt in personal danger, because he believed God would keep and protect him.

While Hugh was tripping over the rubbish that lay around cardboard city, I was stumbling over a pram, cot, and all the other bits and pieces we had acquired since Paul was born. I have a theory that baby things spread to fill all available space. And our little house had reached that stage. We had bought it believing that we'd never have children, and we'd bought it on the strength of Hugh's salary when he was working with The Talbot Association. Now we had a child and we didn't have the same income. Something had to be done. Mum came to the rescue. But how different was my return then to the many times I'd crawled back home during my time with George. This was a happy move and our months with Mum did me good. She was a great support, and she and Paul loved each other.

Then God provided for us in a totally unexpected way. My brother John, who then lived alone, offered to buy and share a home with us. His work involved a lot of travelling, and that arrangement would allow him to have a home base. A suitable house was found and it was our home for the next four years.

'I was stopped by some girls on the street tonight, Maureen,' Hugh told me in the wee hours of one morning when he came home from work. (He went out at 8pm and was usually home between 3 and 6am) 'They were just young girls and they asked if I had any hot soup or tea.'

'What were they doing out in the middle of the night?' I asked.

'They were prostituting.' Hugh shook his head. 'I'll never forget them,' he went on, 'young lassies with just scanty clothes on and blue with the cold.'

'Did you have soup for them?'

'There was some in the flask. I left it with them.'

It was as though a cloud had descended. Neither of us slept well.

Breakfast next morning was a serious business. We had much to talk about.

'It's asking a lot, Maureen,' Hugh concluded, 'But I think it would be wise if you were to be with me when I'm seeing the girls on the streets.'

I could appreciate what he was saying.

'It would only take one person to start a rumour and the Mission's credibility would be under attack.'

'I suppose now that Mum's living with us we could sometimes leave Paul with her during the nights. He usually sleeps right though, so it wouldn't be too much for her.'

Hugh agreed. 'I wouldn't ask you if Mum weren't here,' he said. 'If she could look after Paul one or two nights each week you could come out as a volunteer with me.'

It made good sense. We both felt the desperate need there was to help these girls.

It was a freezing cold winter's night when I first went out on night patrol.

'Put on all the layers you can,' Hugh advised.

I smiled down at my much expanded girth. 'I look like the Mitchelin Man!'

But all my clothes seemed to make little impact on the bitter night air.

'We'll go down to Anderson first,' Hugh told me as he started the engine, 'to one of the nicer skippers.'

Having parked the van, we gathered together flasks and food and set off. 'Follow me,' he said, heading for the underparts of a huge sprawling building. 'I'll shine my torch ahead to see where I'm going and you shine yours on my feet and follow closely. The ground is pockmarked with holes and you'll need to be careful.'

I must have looked dubious.

'Follow my footsteps, he insisted, 'and you'll be alright.'

We made our way inside.

I had absolutely no idea what my surroundings were as we walked further and further under the building. It was darkest dark. Then in the blackness little flickers of light appeared, to my right and left and some in front of me. I could hardly believe what I was seeing. We had entered another world, and I was suddenly overwhelmed with a terrible sadness at the very thought that this was someone's home.

'John!' Hugh called.

'Is that you, Shug?'

'Yes, it's me.'

We made our way to a candlelit corner, to a room and kitchen made entirely of flattened cardboard boxes, John's home. The living room, within its cardboard walls, housed an old seat, an upturned orange box served as his table and that's where the candle stood, alongside a cup, tobacco tin and cigarette papers. At the 'door' of his living room, John had laid a huge foot shaped sponge bathmat with 'Welcome' on it. It was exactly the same as one Mum had bought for Paul. I laughed at the thought.

'Wipe yer feet before ye come inside ma hoose,' John told me.

My laughter felt as though it had been slapped away. This was for real. I wiped my feet and went in. Next door to his living room was John's bedroom, also surrounded by flattened cardboard which reflected grotesquely in the candlelight. There was a mattress on the floor and a beer can stood beside it. On the mattress lay John's dog, his companion and his comfort.

'Whit kin' o' soup is it the nicht, son?' John asked.

'It's good thick lentil soup,' Hugh reassured him.

'That's ma favourite.'

'Who's this wi' ye?' John asked suspiciously.

'This is my wife, John. This is Maureen.'

'Dae you make the soup, Hen?'

I told him I did.

'See this soup,' the man said, 'this soup has saved ma life, Hen. And see aw thae folk there,' he looked around at the flickering candles and hunched figures in the shadows, 'this soup has saved aw their lives as weel.'

I didn't know what to say. But John went on.

'Shug's a great frien' o' mine, and o' aw thae ithers oot there as weel.'

That night, in that situation, I felt utterly inadequate.

'What have you been doing today?' Hugh asked.

John needed no encouragement to speak. He had a sober audience, someone who would listen and give a sensible response.

'A lost ma wife years ago,' John explained, when he felt less suspicious of me. 'An A was left on ma oan. It was the wife who aye payed the bills an' that, and saw tae things in the hoose. Efter she died, A managed fur a wee while, bit then I just couldn'a handle it. I forgot tae pay the bills and then a goat intae debt, then a couldn'a pay them. Efter that I spent ony money A hud on drink just tae shut it aw oot.'

I listened on.

'A'd niver din a washin' in ma life, Hen, and A'd niver yased a sweeper. And when the weans came tae see me they said A was just a tramp, dirty an' aw. They didnae seem to realise A was tryin tae dae ma best. Then they jist stopped comin. A dinnae ken whar they ur. An' ma ain weans dinnae ken where their faither is either, and they dinnae care.'

I had just the very beginnings of understanding why some people ended up sleeping in skippers.

'This is the life A've made for maself, Hen,' John concluded. 'It's aw A can cope wi'. I dinnae want a hoose, wi gas bills and lecky bills. This place'll jist dae me fine.'

Having heard John's story and fed him, we moved on.

John's story was multiplied over and over again in the lives of the people we met that night, men and women. They had come from different backgrounds, some dysfunctional families, some broken families. They included a few who could have done well for themselves, but who's lives had gone pear-shaped. And there were among them some who would never have done very well because they were simple folk, inadequately equipped to deal with life's complexities. The smell of the place they called home was nauseous. Stale alcohol, unwashed bodies and unchanged clothes contributed to a stench that invaded me.

My mind was in overdrive. Hugh wanted me to go out on night patrol with him. We believed God wanted that too. But I had a toddler at home. What might I take home to him? Head lice occurred to me as the least of the likely problems, and my imagination spun with thoughts of scabies, impetigo, and, horror or horrors, that recent scourge, AIDS. But by the end of my first night out with Hugh I knew and he knew without a shadow of a doubt that God's will was for us to work together. We would have to commit Paul to him, and trust our Heavenly Father for protection. But we did take sensible precautions. When we arrived home in the morning we stripped off everything and put our clothes in the washing machine without them touching anything en route. First stop for us was the shower and the bath. Only after that did we look into Paul's bedroom to whisper a good morning to our still sleeping son.

In 1986, we probably saw 30 to 40 people who slept rough in the Anderson area. We also took food (paid for from £30 a month Glasgow City Mission gave us for the purpose) to other places too, bus and train stations were favourites for homeless people. Others slept wherever there was warmth. One of the most pathetic sights I witnessed was people sleeping in narrow lanes on top of hot ventilation grills. Often they slept there in the rain, warm and dry on the underside and soaked through on top. The average age of rough sleepers then was around 40. It is very much younger today. Sometimes we saw couples together, not men with their wives, just couples, companions in drink, clinging to whatever affection they could find in that companionship. Often these women were badly beaten, yet they needed to be wanted. They were locked into relationships that I could begin to understand.

'A'm sick o' him,' a woman in McAslin Street once wept to my mother when I was a girl. She and her children had been thrown out of their home, not for the first time, and Mum had taken them in.

'But whit can A dae. A've naewhaur else tae go and he's Ma man,' she wept through bruise blackened eyes.

I can still picture her children standing round her in our kitchen, traumatised little faces, eyes pinned on their weeping mother, hands clinging to her clothes.

Some of the people I met on night patrol were from that sort of background. And they too had traumatised faces, and they too clung on to whatever affection they could get, even if that affection was liable to turn to violence. But there was a difference. In McAslin Street there was a support structure, it had its own home grown social work department. Neighbours cared for each other as Mum cared for that poor woman.

After doing night patrol, Hugh and I made our way to the girls who prostituted themselves.

'Hello, Shug, how's you?' one of two girls on the street greeted Hugh.

I heard this from the passenger seat of the van.

''What kind of soup is it?'

'Lentil tonight,' Hugh told them.

'Who's the woman in the car, a social worker?'

'No, that's Maureen, my wife.'

I couldn't read what the silence meant. Hugh called me over to be introduced.

'Hello,' both girls said, but there was a definite coolness. Hugh was very welcome, I most certainly was not. It was confirmation to both of us of the rightness of my being there. Hugh's relationship with them had to be one which was comfortable when I was around.

'You'll have to work at it, Maureen,' Hugh said, when we returned to the van. 'You've got to win the right to their trust.'

It was a number of months later that the breakthrough came, when I took one of the girls to hospital for the results of some serious tests. I had prayed earnestly that God would break down the barrier between us, and it was in that situation of her greatest vulnerability, that the poor girl poured out her story.

'My mum was on the drink,' Catherine explained, 'and the old man was as well. When I was 14 they put me on the street to get money for their drink.'

While she spoke I listened and prayed, praying that I would not register shock at the harrowing story I was hearing.

As we waited for her test results, results that might have told Catherine that she had a terminal illness, she opened up further. 'What'll happen to my weans if I die?' she asked. She was about 30 years old.

I thought about her children and remembered my first meeting with them. It was in the early hours of a morning when I had met Catherine at her usual corner in the street, very drunk and hardly able to stand. We sat down on a wall and talked. That night I helped her home, half carrying her up to her flat at the top of a multistorey building. Pushing the flat door open to help her in, I was met by four frightened faces. Her children, aged from 6 to 14 were sitting up in the middle of the night watching television. Their father was in prison. I made tea for Catherine and collected some food from the car for the children. The packet of chocolate biscuits disappeared like snow off a wall. That was the first of many nights spent in that sad home.

Catherine's test was negative. She was going to be alright.

'Will you not try to stop drinking?' I begged her.

'You don't understand,' she said over and over again, 'you just don't understand what it's like.'

'But I do,' I reminded her. 'I've been there, Catherine, I've tried to drown all my sorrows in drink and it just doesn't work.'

She shook her head sadly. 'I know.'

'Will you not try for the children's sakes?' I went on.

'I love my weans,' she said defiantly, 'and I want them to have all the things I've never had. That's why I go out on the street and drink so that it doesn't hurt as much.'

But the truth was that her children saw little of what she earned. When her husband was not in prison he was quite happy for Catherine to prostitute herself, then he drank what she brought in. When he was, it was the only means she had of keeping her children together. Fourteen years on, two of her daughters are heroin addicts and prostitutes, and one son is in prison. All four are deeply scarred by their upbringing. Catherine is no longer on the streets and she is still trying to give up drink. She sees herself as utterly worthless. Catherine's needs are so deep that no human can fill them, only God can.

When we first began the work, most prostitutes were 30 or older. Things have changed. Now most are young girls, many in their teens, some not even school leaving age. At the other end of the scale there are women prostituting themselves who are in their fifties, one even in her sixties. One of the most concerning aspects of our work with these girls over the years is the increase in drug use. The other is the spectre of AIDS. Although Hugh and I had been alcoholics, drug addiction was new to us. It brought new demands, new challenges and new horrors. The first time we found a girl who had overdosed, she still had the needle in her groin. Recognising the urgency of the situation, we put her in the back of the van and drove straight to the nearest hospital. She survived, just. Sadly that was only the first of many such incidents. When we realised that this was going to become a feature of our work we approached the management of a local hospital and asked if they could give us some support. They provided us with training in resuscitation, and so saved lives.

Hugh and I became increasingly aware of the need to have a medical service right there on the streets where the problems were. After some months of discussion we were asked to a meeting in the hospital at which we were given the opportunity to put forward our case. Although we were in uncharted waters, we felt confident in our proposition that if a service were not provided drug deaths on the street would increase alarmingly. Eventually it was decided that a small night clinic would be opened in Waterloo Street, in the red light district of Glasgow. This was an innovation for the Health Board. The clinic has done real pioneer work, but it has opened a can of worms, showing up all sorts of needs that have yet to be met.

Girls who prostitute themselves are open to the most appalling abuse. This has become more of a problem since those with a drug habit to feed have had to become less choosy about their clients. Thankfully most liaisons take place in cars or up city lanes, not many girls trust men enough to go away with them, even to go indoors. Sometimes this saves lives. One night Hugh and I heard a scream from a narrow lane. We ran in the direction of the noise, arriving just in time to see a blade being plunged into the back of a girl's neck, withdrawn and raised for another lunge. We screamed as we'd never screamed before. The man scrambled to his feet and raced off in the opposite direction. This happened before the days of mobile phones. While I stayed with the girl, Hugh ran to the nearest phone box to summon help. By God's grace the girl was saved, had the man been able to entice her indoors she would almost certainly have been murdered. Men like that are filled with a vicious lust that drives them to do the most despicable things.

I once saw a television programme in which three girls who prostituted themselves were interviewed. Their lifestyles were depicted as luxurious. They had given up their day jobs and worked from homes which were rich with material possessions. This cuts right across our experience. Our girls are not on the street to make a good living, as a rule they are there to feed their drug habit. There are exceptions. One girl we met, and who was on the street for about nine months, was a student who prostituted herself to pay her way through university. God help us if that is the way our society is going. Neither of us has ever met a woman on the street who said she enjoyed what she was doing or wanted to continue.

When we first started doing this work, I often cried myself to sleep or couldn't get to sleep at all. But I soon became aware that if we were to have an effective ministry I had to find some way of unburdening, tears and sleepless nights wouldn't help anyone. God's Word is so practical. Paul wrote, 'The Lord is near. Do not be anxious about anything, but in everything, by prayer and petition, with thanksgiving, present your requests to God. And the peace of God, which transcends all understanding, will guard your hearts and your minds in Christ Jesus' (Phil. 4:5-7).

These were truths I had to learn over and over again.

The Lord is near. When Hugh and I go out in the streets, we are never alone. God is with us.

We have no need to be anxious about anything. Our cares are God's cares and he is more than able to bear them.

We have had to learn to take everything to God in prayer, with thanksgiving. Thanksgiving? Were there things we met for which we could give thanks? Yes, there were many. And who knows the outcome of the relationships we make and the conversations we have. God can still bless them.

And the incomprehensible peace of God guards our hearts and minds in Christ Jesus. We could become weighed down and depressed by what we see and hear. But, while it does distress us and we do shed many tears, God has graciously kept our hearts and minds from harm. If we were to take our eyes off him and allow the devil to fill our minds with the horrors we have seen and weigh down our hearts with the sorrow of it all, we would be no use whatsoever.

God made that promise, and he keeps it.

6

History lesson

'Look at them,' Jean commented, as we passed through Glasgow's Blythswood Square, 'They're disgusting.'

'Imagine selling yourself on the street to dirty old men,' I said, turning very obviously away from the women on the pavement, and speaking loudly enough that I knew they could hear me.

Jean snorted. 'They must be desperate!'

Sniggering at the thought we walked on, leaving two young women about our ages to ply their trade.

If I had known in my teens what I knew in my forties, I would not have been so cruel.

A girl who prostitutes herself has a history. Imagine this is yours.

Preschool: you are an unwanted child who receives very little care and attention. Your father has left the scene and your mother is a drug addict. You are made to feel that you are just an inconvenience. Mum often has friends round, so many friends that there is almost a party atmosphere. But things always get unpleasant when the drugs kick in. Like every other child, you crave love and affection. Very little comes from Mum, so you try her friends. Some of them pay attention to you, two of your 'uncles' in particular like to play with you. But the games are not always nice. You see things that children should never see and that you don't know the words to describe ... then these things happen to you. You find yourself in a terrible situation. Because of what is happening to you, you desperately need love, but the people who show you love also hurt you. Then you need even more understanding and care, but it all turns in on itself until you are spinning in a cycle that has no way out. Your 'uncles' tell you that what they do to you is special, and you've to keep it secret. But who would you tell anyway?

Starting school: All the other children in your class seem to be met after school by their dads or mums. On your first day you wait, thinking that Mum must be coming for you. She doesn't. Your teacher notices you standing in the playground after all the others have left. She suggests you wait inside the door with her until Mum comes. But you won't go, you don't want to be alone with her. Grown-ups do such cruel things when you are alone with them. You run away from her and find your own way home. But Mum's not there and the door is locked. You sit on the landing outside the door and wait. When she comes home some hours later you are leaning against the door, having cried yourself to sleep.

Infant school: You don't do well and you think that the pupils and teachers don't like you. You might be right. Because the parents of some of the pupils know your background their children are not encouraged to play with you, and you are certainly never invited to their homes. You don't take friends home, and you wouldn't want to. When things upset you, you say things you hear at your Mum's parties, thinking you are being grown up. Then the children tell their parents what you've said, and are told you are a bad girl. As Mum's friends always seem to be in your house, you rarely have your homework done. And sometimes you are so sleepy that you doze off in class. You are afraid of adults, teachers included. The grown-ups in your home life have inflicted such hurt that you don't trust them or any others. You become furtive in your dealings with adults, and any close contact they have with you makes you freeze. The abuse goes on.

Junior school: You are ashamed of what you are wearing. You've learned how to use the washing machine, so you keep you clothes clean, but you can't iron very well. And Mum doesn't always buy you clothes when you need them, or shoes. You learn to play the survival game, smiling when you are unhappy, cocky when you are hurt. You learn not to cry. When you realise what is happening to you, and what your 'uncles' are doing, apprehension and fear become your companions.

Aged 11 - 12: To cover the humiliation you often feel, you put on a hard face. You are picked on constantly, both at home and at school. School work is a real problem, basic things like reading and writing. Even your communication skills are poor, after all, what good has communicating ever done you? You begin to notice the signs of growing up, but you are not the only one who sees changes in you. Having thought that nothing worse could happen to you, you discover it can when one of your 'uncles' rapes you. You've seen people having intercourse on television many times, nobody ever stopped you watching, Mum's friends sometimes watched with you, but being raped wasn't like that. It was brutal. You want to die.

Aged 13: Something wonderful happens. One of Mum's friends or someone where you live gives you cannabis. When you take it you are flooded with a warm glow, a glow that shuts out what's happening to you and around you. What a relief! Suddenly you know you can handle life. Cannabis allows you to escape when things are awful, and it lets you forget all the things you are afraid of. Mum's friends supply you with cannabis, that's not a problem.

Teenage years: As your need to escape grows, so does you need for cannabis. Mum's friends now want paid when they supply you. You look around for a job you can do, missing school in the process, but nobody wants to employ a known addict's daughter, and a glazed-eyed one at that. Shop-lifting provides you with enough money for a time, then other petty crimes. But your drug habit has changed, cannabis no longer takes away all your hurts and pain, only heroin does that. And heroin is not cheap. Try as you might, you can't get together enough money to feed your habit. The pusher who supplies you tells you of an easy way to earn enough, assures you that he'll arrange it. He does, and having had your innocence taken from you by force as a child, you sell what's left, you sell yourself, and you do it several times a night. You prostitute yourself to pay for your heroin, and you take more heroin to cut out the hurt of it all.

Angela's story
I met Angela when she was in her early twenties. She was a prostitute, a heroin addict and very ill. Her boyfriend had died from a drug overdose two years before we met, leaving her shattered. Angela's story was not much different from what you have just read. She felt that nobody cared, and she didn't care whether she lived or died. A beautiful girl, Angela had a halo of golden curls and large blue eyes. When she laughed, her eyes almost disappeared, swallowed by the radiance of her smile. She was a sweet-natured girl.

After a long struggle, we managed to help Angela to get off the street and into a drug rehabilitation centre where she did really well. It was such a joy to visit her 'Come and see,' she would say excitedly when we arrived, and we would be taken to admire what she had being doing that day. Having come from a background where domestic skills were given no priority, she took great pleasure in learning to bake and to do other homemaking jobs. 'Will you keep praying for me?' Angela always asked when the time came for us to leave. The difference in her life was amazing, but she knew that she wasn't out of the woods. We prayed with her often and told her of the love of Jesus. Angela always responded warmly.

Some months after coming off drugs, Angels moved to another rehabilitation centre. Tragically, someone in the centre had drugs and, in a moment of weakness, our young friend took some.

'Angela is very ill,' a voice told me on the phone one afternoon.

'She's left the centre,' was the message the following morning.

Hugh and I spent most of the day trying to find her. In the evening the phone rang again.

'I'm a friend of Angela,' a girl told us. 'She wants me to give you a message.'

I waited, hoping this would be an address where we could find her.

'She says she can't face cold turkey, she can't go through another recovery. She's too tired and too ill to do that.'

The phone rang off, only to ring again in the early hours of the morning.

'Hello, it's Angela,' said a tremulous voice.

'Where are you?' I asked gently. 'Do you want us to come for you?'

It was as though she had not heard what I was saying.

'I just want to thank both of you,' our dear young friend went on. 'Nobody ever loved me before. I'm awful sorry I took a hit but it was available, and I just did. And I don't want to go on living. I got my test results yesterday, it was positive.'

She didn't need to explain. Positive, HIV positive, the spectre of AIDS was what the girl was facing.

Angela went on. 'I don't want to make any more trouble for you, but please keep on doing what you're doing for the sake of all the others. It doesn't matter about me now, but keep fighting for them.'

There was a long pause.

'I love you both very much,' Angela's voice broke, 'and I hope there's a place in heaven for me.'

'Please tell me where you are,' I begged, my heart breaking at what was happening.

Angela blew a kiss down the phone.

'Bye bye,' she cried at the other end.

And the line went dead.

'I can't do this work,' I wept to Hugh, when we heard of Angela's death from a deliberate overdose a short time later. 'I'm just not able for it.'

My husband was also in tears, his heart was broken too. We talked about it and prayed about it and got up and got on. In fact, I became an employee of Glasgow City Mission rather than a volunteer. We knew we were trusted by so many needy people, and we couldn't leave them in the lurch. God used their needs to keep us in the work. I now believe that when our hearts don't break when one of our friends dies, that will be the time to resign.

'Let's stop here a minute,' Hugh said, as we drove along Holm Street just a few weeks later. 'We'll go over and look at that shop.'

We parked the van, got out and crossed the road to an empty shop in a fairly derelict block and peered through the window.

'It's a mess inside,' I announced.

'That's because it's been empty for years,' my husband told me. 'It used to be a trophy shop.'

Having had a good look, we went back to the van.

'It would make a great place for the women and girls to come to, somewhere they could feel safe, and not far from where most of them work,' I said.

This was our dream. As we worked that night, we discussed the possibility. Agreeing that the location was good and the need was urgent, we decided to approach Mr Macdowell, the Mission's Superintendent.

'A project like this needs a Board decision,' he told us. 'I'll arrange for you to meet them and you can present your case. You've certainly made a good case to me.'

Hugh and I did our homework and were well prepared for the Board meeting.

'It is a very big outlay,' one member commented.

'We have worked out an annual running cost of about £1400,' Hugh told them, explaining how we had reached that figure.

It was agreed that a decision would be made at their next meeting, three months later.

That night we met with a group of friends who were committed to praying for our work in a very intimate and informed way.

'... so,' concluded Hugh, when he had told them about the rooms in Holm Street, 'please pray that the Lord will lead the Board to come to the right decision, and guide us to know if this is what we should be working towards.'

He made no mention of the sum of money required. We were always careful not to cross the boundaries of confidentiality between the Board and our prayer supporters.

'I'd like you to use this in the work,' one of our friends said as she was leaving. She handed Hugh an envelope.

'Maureen,' he said, when we were alone and he'd had time to look at the contents. 'It seems the Lord is telling us he wants us to have these rooms.'

Hugh handed me our friend's cheque. It was a donation of £1400 towards our work. My heart soared!

Three months later (though it seemed much longer!) we received the Board's permission to proceed, and the City Council raised no objections. Cleaning began, and that was quite some job. What a wonderful group of folk volunteered to roll up their sleeves and help.

'It'll be great to be able to come to the rooms for a cup of tea in the winter,' girls told us when they called in to see what we were doing. We had not really considered what to call the premises. The Rooms it was.

'Would a retired post bus be any use to you?' my brother John asked one day.

Hugh was quick to imagine its usefulness. 'It certainly would,' he replied.

John was pleased. 'I think I can arrange that for you.'

When the newspapers reported the opening of The Rooms on 5th August, 1991, the photo also showed the car keys being handed over. A new phase in our work had begun.

While Hugh and I had been aware of the need to have a drop-in centre, we had not realised how fully it would be used. Women and girls who worked in the streets came in for warmth and comfort. And families, often the subject of abuse and violence, sought refuge in The Rooms.

Help came to us from unexpected quarters.

'I'd like to do something to help with the work,' one of the city's top bakers told us. 'Is there anything you're needing?'

We thought about it.

'For example,' he went on, 'when you're out on the streets what do you do for toilet facilities and the like?'

Hugh admitted that could be a problem.

'I tell you what,' the man smiled. 'You know my city centre shop?'

I nodded.

'Well, I'll have keys made for you and you can use the facilities there. And I'll get the staff to leave out all the left-over bakery. You'll be able to make use of it in The Rooms. And there's a glass cake display cabinet you can have too.'

After his shop closed each day, we went there and collected wooden boards full of the best bakery that Glasgow could supply. How good God is. He didn't only provide enough for the girls who dropped into The Rooms, he provided the very best. Many people regard our girls as the lowest of the low, to my shame that was what I thought when I was young, but God loves them and provided the very best for them. It is because Hugh and I believe that he also provided Jesus as their Saviour that we do the work we do, and why we held a Bible Time each night in The Rooms. What a difference premises made to our work. Hugh continued doing night patrol as before, and I stayed at The Rooms with other women volunteers and cared for those who dropped in there. Pixie was among those who came.

Pixie's story

Although Pixie, who was less than five feet tall and in her late twenties, was a pretty girl, she always looked as though she was going to cry. She had one of the saddest expressions I've ever known. Her dark brown eyes seemed sunken and her thin lips were often blue with cold. When Pixie entered The Rooms she was always hunched up, only when the heat relaxed her did she uncurl and sit upright. This young woman lived with a man who manipulated her in every way, including forcing her to sell herself on the streets to finance his drug habit.

'He'd murder me,' she told me quietly and sincerely, 'he'd murder me if I tried to get away.'

Pixie was easy to be with. I gave her all the silence she needed, only that allowed her to talk.

'Don't think I've not tried it,' she said. 'I have and I'm lucky to be alive.'

I often asked Pixie to stay for Bible Time, and she seemed to enjoy doing that. At first only a few stayed out of curiosity, but eventually women and girls started coming in just at that time and it got busier and busier. We were often asked very challenging questions.

'Some men came to Jesus,' Hugh told our girls one night 'and they brought with them a woman who had been caught in the act of adultery. They were all prepared to stone her to death which was what the law allowed, but before they did they tried to catch Jesus out by asking him if he thought that the law's punishment was just. Instead of answering them right away, Jesus wrote something in the sand with his finger. The men continued to badger him for an answer. Jesus stood up, "If any one of you is without sin," he said, "let him be the first to throw a stone at her." Having silenced them, he again wrote in the sand. Instead of stoning the woman, her accusers slunk away, first one, then another then another. Only when they had all gone did Jesus look up at the woman. "Where are they?" he asked her, looking round for the men. "Has no-one condemned you?" She answered that no-one had. "Then neither do I condemn you," Jesus told her. "Go now and leave your life of sin"' (from John 8:3-11).'

There was silence in The Rooms as the girls and women took in what Hugh was saying. He didn't fudge around the fact that adultery is sin, but it seemed that there was hope in what Jesus told the guilty woman. That was a solemn evening in The Rooms. Bible Time that night lasted longer than usual, well over an hour, as questions and discussions and quiet conversations followed. It was also an hour that these girls were not on the streets. Pixie spoke to me afterwards, with tears in her eyes. All she wanted was to go home to a secure home and a happy one, but what she was being forced to do was to go back out into the streets and sell herself.

Many of these girls had no settled homes, and no long term relationships far less husbands. They moved between houses and hostels, anywhere where they could find heat and shelter. Inevitably some became pregnant. Sadly abortion was seen as the easy way out, though a number gave birth to children. To my horror, I have to say that new mothers were usually back on the streets almost immediately after childbirth. One girl, out of her mind with desperation for heroin, had her baby one morning and prostituted herself that night. Often babies were taken into care, but sometimes their mothers kept them, deluded into thinking that they could cope with their infants and continue the lives they were leading. Our girls have the same emotional needs as any others, including the need to love and care for their own children. Sadly, that kind of thinking is not in the real world. From time to time I have been in attendance when the decision was taken to take a child from its mother and put it into care. My job was to do what I could for the bereft young mothers, and they were bereft. But I also thought of my dear Paul, sound asleep in his little bed with his granny looking after him.

Our ministry extended to the men, like Pixie's partner, who forced girls on to the street to bring money back for their drug habits. At first I rebelled against helping them. Were they not the ones who were to blame for the heartbreak we so often met on the street? I had to think that one through. The truth is that the people who benefit are not addicts at all. There are those who gain vast sums of money from drugs and never as much as smoke cannabis. They live in absolute luxury, employing others to do their dirty work. There are several tiers in the system, and many tears at the bottom of it. The men who send girls out are, in their own way, abused by the pushers who supply them with their drugs. Most pushers are themselves addicts and it is only when you go above that tier that you reach those who make a conscious decision to exploit drugs without being users themselves. Sadly, those who are caught and imprisoned are usually among the addicts rather than the businessmen.

Glasgow City Mission at that time had several Mission Halls that were greatly used by the Lord to minister to Glasgow's disadvantaged people. Hugh and I often visited the Maryhill Mission Hall, and there we met the most amazing people. The women, for example, made huge pans of mince and potatoes every Thursday, to minister to those in need of comfort and food. And there we met men like Wee Robbie. Robbie, a converted alcoholic, never missed an opportunity to speak to people about the Lord in his Glasgwegian, no holds barred, straight off the shoulder, way. He even came out on night patrol with us when he was able. When I met Robbie for the last time, it was in an oncology unit where he was receiving treatment for throat cancer. Although he could not speak, his expression left me in no doubt that he was sure God was right there with him. Robbie is now in glory with his beloved Lord. My life was enriched by the times I spent with him, and by his simple, direct and urgent faith.

Robbie, like Hugh and me, was a prisoner of sin and a slave to alcohol. We were saved by Jesus Christ, not by anything in us or anything we could do. The people we meet on the streets are as we were. Perhaps that is why the Lord has given us this ministry to do. We can never say that we don't understand addiction, we can stand with our folk and say that we do understand and that there is a way out.

7

Cornerstone

We read the letter sadly, and read it over and over again. It was not a surprise, but it was perplexing.

'Where will the girls go when The Rooms close down?' I asked Hugh. 'They need to have somewhere. Surely God didn't open up this work just to have it brought to an end because the Council has decided to demolish the building.'

Hugh was deep in thought, probably in prayer.

'Think of Margaret Taylor,' I went on. 'Where will she be without The Rooms. She still needs a place like that to go to.'

Hugh nodded. He's known me long enough to recognise the times when I need to let off steam and he leaves me to get on with it. This was one of them.

'Did The Rooms change Margaret?' he asked, when I came to an end. Hugh's voice was quiet, a sure sign that I needed to think hard about what he was saying.

'No,' I acknowledged. 'Only God could do that, but The Rooms certainly helped.'

'And does God change with circumstances?' my husband persevered.

'He's the same yesterday, today and forever,' I

admitted, quoting one of my favourite verses from the Bible.

Hugh relaxed. 'The Rooms may close,' he said, 'but God still loves these girls and still wants us to reach out to them. It's the work that's important, Maureen, not where it's done.'

As the date drew near for The Rooms to close, we made a conscious effort to count our blessings, the blessings that had come as a result of having a place where women, girls and sometimes families could find refuge and help. And we prayed that if God wanted us to continue providing a place of safety, he would lead us to find suitable premises. The problem was that our work was based in Glasgow's Anderson district, to move out of that area would mean abandoning those whom we had been working with, and starting all over again. More importantly, Anderson was probably the worst of the city's red light districts, and we believed God was calling us to remain there.

The clock was ticking relentlessly towards the time for The Rooms' final closing when Hugh asked if I had noticed the vacant public house at the other end of the block of which The Rooms were part, but outwith the area for demolition. We went along and had a look.

'We've often looked through the gloom into pubs,' I commented, thinking back to our past years, 'but never quite like this.'

Hugh laughed as we rubbed the dust from the outside of the window and peered through the glass into the long narrow interior, bar fittings intact and all. 'It would be ironical if a place like this was used to help folk kick their addictions,' he said. 'What do you think?'

I applied myself to as thorough a viewing as was possible through the dirty glass. A bar ran the length of the room, shelves ranged behind it, empty of the glasses and bottles they would once have held. The seating bays were laid out in semicircles.

'It's certainly big enough,' I said, 'and that arrangement of seats would allow for small groups to have private conversations.'

'There will be toilets too,' Hugh pointed out, 'and other back premises.'

I looked at my husband. 'Do you really think the Lord would use an old public house to provide a refuge for folk with addiction problems?'

He smiled mischievously. 'It would need to be converted first,' he said, 'just like us.'

We prayed about it, we discussed it with Glasgow City Mission's Board, who agreed to an application being sent to the City Council. How thankful we were to God when we eventually held the keys of the public house in our hands. It was time for its conversion.

A willing group of volunteers, from different churches and denominations, gave their time and energy to the job. And it thrilled our hearts that Margaret and Gregor, two souls whom God had graciously rescued through the ministry, rolled up their sleeves and worked tirelessly for nearly a month to make our new premises habitable. When

111

we took the place over, it stank of nicotine and alcohol. Cleaning the walls and floor was more a case of scraping than scrubbing, and each layer that came off seemed to expose more of the pervasive odour that anyone who has frequented a public house will know. Even the pipes running under the bar seemed to be coated with the smell of whisky.

The provision of new premises came just when we needed it, and just when Margaret and Gregor needed it too, but for quite a different reason. They had both been addicts and were now well on the road of recovery. God so timed things that when they most needed to have their time taken up and their minds occupied with thoughts other than of drugs, they had no time to spare and no energy either. They worked their hearts out, and they worked their problems out, with sugar soap, steel wool and elbow grease. When the place was cleaned, painted and sporting a warm red carpet, it looked well and truly converted. The premises needed a name, and we puzzled over several. But one day, as I was driving home from work, the Lord seemed to give me the name Cornerstone. It was just right. Jesus is the cornerstone of our faith, and Cornerstone we hoped and prayed would be used to bring many people to faith in him.

We opened five nights a week, Monday to Friday, serving soup, sandwiches and the delicious cakes that our baker friend kindly provided. While women and girls in need were always welcome in Cornerstone, the door was kept locked for safety reasons. Because some of those who used our facilities did so to escape abusers, the door was locked against them. In order for the girls to feel safe, none of them ever opened the door.

When girls came into Cornerstone, they brought with them stories of abuse, heartache, addiction, and despair. The greatest thing we could give them was not warmth or food, but rather the love of our hearts and the embrace of our open arms. That, we believed, was what Jesus wanted us to do. All that we did was just a tiny reflection of his love for these girls. And how they needed it. Of the thirty or so who came to Cornerstone on the average night, some would be prostitutes seeking refuge before selling themselves yet again and enduring they knew not what, others would be wives fleeing violent drunken husbands, some would be homeless and looking for shelter, and perhaps there would be a mother with her children just thrown out on the street.

Amy's story
We had met Amy on the street often over the years. She was just a slim scrap of a girl, a picture of fear and vulnerability. Amy lived with a man who sold her over and again every night to line his pockets and shoot drugs into his veins. Early one evening, when Hugh and I went into a McDonald's for a cup of tea, we met Amy.

'Hello,' she greeted us, as we sat down beside her.

I looked at the girl. 'You're soaked through,' I said, 'will you stay here in the heat until you're dry?'

She shook her head. 'I'm just in for my breakfast.'

Having prostituted herself all of the previous night, she had slept all day. Now she was bracing herself for another night's work with a sweet, creamy milk shake. Girls who follow Amy's lifestyle regularly survive on sweet drinks and the occasional burger. They are often severely malnourished.

Amy shivered despite the heat, her wet clothes still clung to her.

'I wish I was dead,' she sighed.

We sat quietly, giving her space should she want to say more. She did.

'I'm scared stiff, Maureen,' she went on. 'I'm scared not to go out on the streets because Paul would kill me. I'm scared when I go out in case someone else does. And I'm scared to go back in the mornings because it doesn't matter how many men I go with and what they do to me, I can never earn enough to please him.'

Rising to her feet, Amy pulled her skimpy damp clothes about her and left, to satisfy the lust of her partner for heroin, and to fail yet again. But she was locked in. Amy had no way out. Our hearts ached as we watched her go.

There were nights when I went home and just hung my head and confessed to God how *utterly helpless I felt in relation to Amy. And that feeling of helplessness is exhausting. Over and again we tired ourselves out in the work we were doing, there seemed to be no end of need. It was almost as though a cry went up from the Anderson area as it grew dark each night, a cry we did our best to answer. But sometimes I felt that I was trying to mop up a whole sea of sadness and hurt with a paper handkerchief.*

In January 1992, not long after we met Amy in McDonald's, she was found dead in a railway station toilet. Such deaths were not unusual, but each was horrifyingly tragic. When a girl died, the others organised a collection for the next of kin, usually the children. But Amy had no children and there was no question of giving money to the man who had used and abused her for so long. Instead, a painting was bought for our premises and it hung there in memory of Amy. It depicts a peaceful scene of hill and loch. A flock of sheep are in the background, but in the foreground a sheepdog is nudging a stray lamb back to the flock. That picture is symbolic of the work we do.

Glasgow's night life underwent a change in the early nineties and we began to see girls in their early teens on the streets. Similarly with homelessness, in our early days most homeless people were men, the traditional two-coaters, but within ten years there was a lowering of the age of those staying in cardboard city. Teenage boys and girls became the norm and nobody, it seemed, blinked an eye. Many of these young folk were from second generation drug addicted families. That was the environment in which they had been raised, and that was really all they knew. Many times I've been told that these kids deserve what has come to them. My reply is that that statement is made in ignorance of the facts. If those who say that kind of thing knew what most of these young people had gone through before finding themselves on the streets they would be more compassionate and far less critical.

We were horrified when we started to meet prostitutes as young as 14 and 15. The older women generally let us know when a girl that age appeared on the scene. They knew all the dangers of prostitution, and not one of them wanted a young girl involved. Many times we have called in the social services stand-by service for young girls and boys. Most of them were from disturbed backgrounds, some had run away from foster homes or children's homes. We longed to be able to do something for these children, and that is what they are, just children, but our hands were tied and our every working hour was full to capacity.

Sophie, Marlyn and Helen's story
'Hello,' the Cornerstone volunteer said to the three young girls who made their way in.
'Hello,' all three said, trying to stifle their giggles.

I looked at them. They were just girls.

Taking their tea and cakes over to them, I sat down and chatted. It wasn't long before their stories tumbled out.

'Do you come from this part of the city?' I asked.

They dissolved in laughter.

'No,' one explained, 'but we come in here because this is where all the action is. There's nothing doing in the scheme where we live.'

'Tell me about yourselves,' I invited.

'I'm Sophie and I'm 16,' the first one said, 'and these are Marlyn and Helen. They're ancient. They're 17!'

Another fit of giggles followed. It took some time to subside.

But before the evening was through, I knew much more about them. All three came from dysfunctional families, two had alcoholic fathers and the third's mother was the same. All had stopped attending school regularly when they were aged about 13, and all had been in and out of care. Their giggles rang hollow as time went on. By the end of the evening each had shed tears as they shared some of what they had gone through.

There were times when I took on the role of a mother and spoke very seriously, especially to the younger girls, about what could happen to them if they continued to hang about our area of town at night time. This was one such

*occasion. Painting a picture of street life as I
saw it, I explained the dangers graphically.*

*'That won't happen to us,' Helen said. 'We
know how to look after ourselves. And we're in
it together, we'll keep an eye on each other.'*

*The three came back to Cornerstone from
time to time, and I always reiterated my
warnings if they gave me the opportunity. I think
it reassured them that I cared.*

*Their story has a tragic ending. The girls
went to a party, no doubt keeping an eye on
each other, but Sophie mixed alcohol with drugs
and was found dead the following morning,
choked on her vomit. I prayed that her tragic
death would bring the other two to their senses,
but it did not. They got deeper and deeper into
the lifestyle. Just a few months later, Helen died
in not dissimilar circumstances. I wonder what
the future holds for Marlyn, or if she has one.*

In the mid nineties there was a spate of murders is
our area of the city. The victims were prostitutes
and they were all known to us. The atmosphere in
Anderson at that time was surreal. For three or four
nights after each murder the streets were eerily
quiet, but by the end of the week it was back to
business as usual. Such was the desperation of these
girls for heroin, or such was their fear of those who
manipulated them, that they went back on the
streets prostituting themselves with potential
murderers.

Cornerstone was more than usually busy then. Girls huddled round each other and talked quietly. They voiced the hope that it would never happen to them, but in their hearts they feared they would be next, that the Police incident caravan would move down the street to their patch. I could write a whole book about the events surrounding those murders, but it would do no good. The girls are dead. But something has to be said, and it seems to me to be this. There are girls and boys, women and men prostituting themselves on the streets of every town and city in the country. Most come from backgrounds we can't begin to imagine. Many were victims of all kinds of abuse before they ever had their first smoke of cannabis or taste of alcohol. There is nothing romantic about their situation, it cannot be presented in any way that is palatable or attractive. It is therefore at the bottom of the charity stakes. How much easier it is to have compassion on a wide-eyed starving baby in the Sudan, or a child from a Brazilian shanty town, or an amputee crippled by a land mine in Bosnia, than on a teenaged drug addict and prostitute in the town where we live. If that is how we react, we have serious questions to ask ourselves regarding the extent of our compassion and the fullness of the Lord's.

Although we saw much sadness in the course of our work, there were many happy times too. Each year we held an open air carol service just before Christmas. At it we served soup and hot chocolate and all sorts of goodies. Our homeless friends and many of the street girls came to the service. And it is only in eternity that we will know if hearts were touched by the reminder of the birth of the infant Saviour. Several Glasgow churches donated gifts and toys to Glasgow City Mission and these were distributed to children for whom Christmas might otherwise have passed by unmarked. We put on a family treat each year in Cornerstone, ranging from a traditional party to a puppet performance.

Of course Cornerstone could only function thanks to the volunteers who committed themselves to the work there. In the early months of the venture we had about 30, but that number rose to between 70 and 80. These men and women were totally committed to the cause. They had to be. However, not everyone who volunteered was a suitable helper. Some who offered their services had problems of their own that needed to be resolved before they could be of real help. We cannot carry our own baggage into work of this kind, we have to be able to leave our personal concerns behind and concentrate only on the problems we meet in the work. Volunteers were trained before they started, and relationships monitored on an on-going basis. It was our practice to pray for each other and to resolve any ripples before they grew big enough to become difficulties. This kind of staff management was a whole new area for Hugh and me. To say it was a steep learning curve only begins to describe it.

Emma's story

Our volunteer helpers often saw city life in the raw for the very first time when they came to work with us. Thankfully they were rewarded with great blessings as well as challenged by terrible pain. Emma is one of our blessings. Having come from a sad background she sought love in a relationship with a boy who was on drugs. When she started coming to Cornerstone she was a young teenager and homeless, he was a little older. Emma was very naive, with the kind of naivety that doesn't survive life on the streets. She went with her boyfriend to a party, a party where plenty of drugs were in evidence. The girl genuinely didn't realise what was going on round about her, so much so that when the police raided the premises and everyone made a run for it, Emma remained to be interviewed by them. To her horror and great confusion, she was charged.

So began yet another learning curve for Hugh and me. By the end of the following year we were quite familiar with the court system, and had become adept at working with social workers, lawyers and probation officers. When her case eventually came to court, after several delays, Emma stood in the dock knowing that she might get a custodial sentence of five or more years. However, we were able to show that she had come to us for support and had made very good use of what help was available.

How we thanked God that the girl was given probation. The judge even wished us well in the work we were doing! Today Emma is getting on fine. She has a home of her own and a small child. We still see her and rejoice in her success.

Two other friends, Margaret and Gregor, who were in at the beginnings of Cornerstone with their sleeves rolled up to scour the place, were integral to the work done there. God is so good.

Glasgow City Mission was constantly surprised by how the work developed and we were grateful for the support we were given. But sometimes things even surprised us. Having come to it as raw amateurs, we found ourselves providing placements for a variety of professional trainings. Anne Kelly, who had welcomed me to church when I went as a new Christian unsure of what to do and when to do it, remained a good friend. When her daughter, who was training to be a social worker, needed to find a placement, Anne suggested she come to us. So helpful was it, and so committed were we to ensuring that professionals really knew what was going on in the city, that our placement programme was set up. And, having had her daughter come as a student, Anne followed, remaining as a valued volunteer.

Not all of Cornerstone's work took place during the hours of darkness. A weekly lunch club opened, where tasty meals were provided. Young women, mums with toddlers, met and enjoyed the facility.

Sausage stew was the favourite item on the menu, and it was followed by a variety of puddings. Food has featured throughout our work. Most of the time it was paid for out of our food allowance. Often it was supplemented by gifts and donations. Occasionally it came as a result of a miracle, right from the hand of God. One January night we had no soup. If was freezing cold and our homeless friends were much in need of the warmth and sustenance soup provided. I went into my office (can you call a 4' by 5' room an office? Yes, if it has a chair and a phone, and mine did!). Having prayed, I was just about to make a phone call to see if I could arrange to get food, when there was a knock on my office window. It was Margaret.

'Come here,' she said, signalling the urgency of it.

I went out.

'Look at this!' announced Margaret excitedly.

A man stood there holding a huge pan of home-made soup!

'My wife made soup enough for a Boy Scout camp!' he laughed. 'There's more than we could ever eat. We thought you might be able to use it.'

Could we!

Glasgow City Mission's work through Cornerstone was blessed. There was nothing whatever we could do that would make an impact on the huge problems in the area in which we worked, but an impact was made, and it was all God's doing. As for Hugh and me, we did our best but we made our mistakes. Thankfully, God graciously allowed us to make our mistakes quietly, in ways that could be used to train us for the work he was planning for our future.

8

At your service

Not far form Cornerstone was another disused public house, and once again Hugh and I found ourselves peering though its window to view its potential. That seems to have become something of a hobby! We were desperately in need of a refuge for men and boys. The women and girls were being quite well served by Cornerstone. Having looked in the window, we looked at each other.

'It's just what we need,' Hugh said.

Our conversation continued with our faces pressed against adjacent windows.

'It's bigger than Cornerstone,'

'Yes, I reckon it would hold 70 to 80 easily.'

'We could leave the bar as a service area.'

'And the seating arrangement is fine too.'

'There must be a lounge underneath ... see, there's an arrow pointing down.'

'We'll have to pray about it.'

But the praying had begun long before we saw those premises. We knew there was a real need for a male refuge. Was this where it was to be?

The Board of Glasgow City Mission agreed to support the project and the City Council backed the idea and gave us the building at a nominal rent.

What we had prayed about and looked towards for years, the Lord provided in an amazingly short space of time. We opened The Refuge four nights a week, from 7.30 - 11.30-12 midnight. This allowed us to reach out to the lonely men we were meeting in increasing numbers. Most evenings we had up to 40 older men and about 30 young men and boys. Business boomed. Had we been a commercial coffee bar and sausage shop we might have made a fortune. But we were a charity, and the souls of those we served were of infinitely more value than any money. The volunteer base built up as did those who supported us in other ways, for example, by giving a gift of many hundreds of sausages on a regular basis! The Lord moved the hearts of butcher and baker and many others besides.

It was a source of concern to us that a number of the people who used The Refuge had serious medical conditions but, because they had no fixed abodes, they were unable to register with a doctor. Nor were they eligible to use hospital Accident and Emergency Departments as their conditions tended to be chronic rather than in need of emergency care. In fact, homeless people are in the main part cut off from medicine, dentistry and other paramedical services. After praying about this and discussing it with the Mission, we approached Glasgow Health Board with the suggestion that they could hold a clinic in the downstairs room of The Refuge. This had formerly been a small family lounge. Officials from the Health Board inspected the premises, then discussed the details of the project. What a wonderful day it was when the news came that they had decided to pilot the project.

The clinic-to-be was whitewashed and furnished with an examination couch, desk, chairs, and filing cabinet, all supplied by the Health Board. Among our volunteers were doctors, nurses, social workers and others whose input was invaluable. And we needed all their expertise. As soon as the clinic opened, Glasgow's bush telegraph went into overdrive and we had more people arriving for medical help than the doctor could possibly cope with. When they arrived, we took their names and did a cursory screening out of those who really needed medical attention and those whose problems were less urgent or could be dealt with by someone else. The doctor who was allocated to us two evenings each week was splendid, an open compassionate man who made his patients feel at ease. They would have been most uncomfortable had they gone to a doctor who wore a suit and tie, ours came in jeans and an casual top. Many of his patients at The Refuge were the worse of drink and / or drugs, but he was kindly and caring in his dealings with them. Although most patients were men, our women and girls used the service too, especially drug users who suffered from appalling abscesses. Several times the clinic turned into an Accident and Emergency Department when boys who had been stabbed were brought in for help. And lives were saved there.

It was when that happened we realised how much we needed a vehicle that could transport a stretcher patient to hospital. At first these were taken by any means available, but something more appropriate was required. Hugh and I approached the Mission. They must have wondered what was coming when we phoned to make an appointment.

'So you see,' Hugh concluded, having described the problem, 'why we are asking you to apply for a Frontera which will double as a workhorse and an ambulance.'

'But that's top of the range,' was the reply.

Hugh nodded. 'I know, but only something like that will go down the gradients and through the mire that leads to skippers and also double as an ambulance when needed.'

'Do you think there is any chance of getting it?' we were asked.

'I think we should try,' I said. 'This is the last year Scottish Television is running Scottish Telethon Appeal so it's our last chance.'

It was agreed to apply, and we still thank God we did. STV send us a cheque to cover the cost and we were able to buy a new Frontera. It has served well since it was bought in 1993.

Before The Refuge opened for the evening, staff and volunteers prepared sandwiches, cooked sausages and whatever else was on the menu, got the doctor's list ready, then we all met for prayer. Often about 25 of us, staff volunteers, gathered to commit the night to the Lord, asking his blessing on all who came in. Most nights upwards of 100 men and boys came through the door.

Chris's story
A good looking boy with a mop of golden curls, Chris had slept rough since his late teens. By the time we met him he had a terrible drug habit, using whatever he could to blot out the memories from which he was trying to escape. He was once brought to Cornerstone with a stab wound which needed urgent hospital attention. When The Refuge opened, Chris used it often.

One night, a girl came running into The Refuge to tell us that Chris was in intensive care. He had been sleeping rough in a flat which had gone on fire. What followed is etched on my memory. We went to the hospital and obtained permission to visit. Chris was on life support. His face was swollen like a huge pumpkin, and his body was horribly swollen too. He was terribly burned. Our young friend had been under the influence of drugs when the fire broke out. It was well established before he was aware that anything was wrong, and by that time the fire had done its awful damage.

As I sat beside him that night, I thought back over Chris's sad life, remembering the stories he had told us of what childhood had been like for him. He had used drugs to try to wipe the hurt from his memory. Now this. If Chris survived, how would he cope? I asked myself.

Hugh and I prayed for him, we surrounded him with our love and willed him to fight on. And he did. We were privileged to be with him as he went through the agonies of drug withdrawal as well as the effects of his burns. The following weeks were terrible for the lad. I have no words to describe them. And though it hurts me to say it, he was not always treated sympathetically by some members of the hospital staff who saw him first as a drug addict then as a burn patient. Hugh and I fought to get the best care for Chris. I don't suppose it occurs to some people that drug addicts have histories, sometimes histories of abuse and hurt going back to their very earliest memories.

Chris remained in hospital and it was our great privilege to minister to him and to his mother and girlfriend too. We had no idea what kind of future the boy would have, or if he would have one, but one thing we did know was that the future of all things and everyone is in the hands of God. As Christians we believed that if Chris were to trust in the Lord Jesus Christ as Saviour, he would have a sure and certain future in heaven regardless of what his time on earth held for him. Over the years we had spoken with the boy about the Lord, and now in hospital he talked more and more about him. He plied us with questions and begged us to pray for him and to help him. His poor scarred body was beyond our help, but we prayed for relief for *his pain and most of all that he would know the peace that passes all human understanding.*

As a result of smoke inhalation Chris's lungs were badly damaged, consequently he suffered from repeated chest infections. More than nine months after the fire, he was still in hospital and was clearly poorly. Each chest infection left him weaker. On an unforgettable visit we found a very different young man in bed. Our friend told us that he had put his trust in the Lord Jesus and that his Saviour had given him peace through and through. Just one week later, the Lord took Chris home to heaven, there to be with him for ever. How comforted we were that he would never again know crying or pain, nor would he shed even one more tear. It was our privilege to be part of that boy's life, to be part of his living and part of his dying.

Jimmy's story

Just occasionally I met my own childhood in the work I was doing, and that happened when one man walked through the door of The Refuge. I thought I knew his face, then I was quite sure I did. It was Jimmy! A memory of McAslin Street came flooding back. It was a hard frosty day and the boys had made a long slide on the slope of the street. They were whizzing down it, each one adding to its slipperiness as he went. John, my brother, was among those who had the courage to go.

'Are you scared to go?' a boy's voice beside me asked.

It was Jimmy. We all knew Jimmy. His parents had been drowned on a boat going to Ireland and Jimmy lived with his granny. He was a simple boy and sadly often laughed at. But he was kind.

'Yes,' I admitted. 'It's miles long and awful slippy.'

'Come on,' he encouraged, 'you can come down with me on my shovel.'

We climbed up the hill to the top of the slide and waited our turn, my heart racing. When the boy before us headed off, I perched with Jimmy on his shovel and we pelted down the slide, exhilarated and speechless at the end of it. And that simple lad, who had helped me to have the courage to do what I could not do myself, was standing in The Refuge in need of our care.

Jimmy told me that he had spent his adult life in a variety of hostels in the Glasgow area. In the course of our work Hugh and I had become familiar with many of them. Some were grim places, cold and cheerless, full of sad, lonely people who had little to look back on and nothing to look forward to. It made me wonder where all the other children were who had played on that slide, and if any more of them were likely to come in needing refuge. Jimmy is still in a hostel, and we keep in touch with him.

The work we did through Glasgow City Mission was, by 1994, extensive. We had two refuges, the street work, night patrol to Anderson's skippers and the clinic too. To help ease the burden the Mission employed two members of staff, Lyn and Ewan. Meanwhile The Refuge launched yet another new venture, a chiropody service. People like Jimmy who lived in hostels, had to be out of them first thing in he morning and were not allowed back until well through the evening, consequently they walked many miles in the course of each day. Because they wore second-hand and usually ill-fitting shoes, their feet got into a terrible mess. We asked the Health Board to consider providing chiropody care and they did so in the form of Jenny Atland. It was a moving sight to see one of our volunteers in a tiny corner of The Refuge, gently prising the shoes off an old man's feet, sometimes the first time they had been off in weeks, and washing his feet tenderly before Jenny applied her services to them. Never, despite the stench, did I see either of them react distastefully. Both did what they did with compassion. The Bible tells of a woman who loved the Lord because he had forgiven all her sins. She wept tears of love and gratitude that fell on to the Lord's feet and washed them, then she dried them with her hair. Her's was a beautiful expression of love. When I saw our dear friends at work on dirty feet, I saw it as a most beautiful act of compassion. And the Bible tells us that what we do for others, we do for Jesus.

We were aware of yet one more medical service that was necessary. None of those who came into The Refuge and few of those who used Cornerstone were registered with a dentist. Dental care came away down their list of priorities, until they were stricken by toothache and had to resort to primitive methods of extraction. Even some of the little children with whom we had to do had teeth that pained them. We pursued the possibilities and the Lord opened the door. Before long, every Tuesday evening a mobile dental unit parked outside The Refuge and took care of the dental needs of those who used our services.

'I can hardly believe this is all happening,' I commented to Hugh, as we walked between Cornerstone and The Refuge.

Hugh nodded his head. He understood. 'It's all of God,' he said. 'We've only been tiny tools in his hands.'

I knew that was true, and it was in the sense of counting our blessings that we talked over the list of the Mission's projects in Anderson.

'There was night patrol, then getting to know the girls who prostitute themselves. Then came The Rooms and all the wonderful things God did there,' said Hugh.

It was my turn to add some blessings and to be thankful for them. 'God provided the old post bus, and the pub to be used as The Refuge.'

Hugh took over. 'And the clinic, the dentist and chiropodist.'

'And don't forget Winnie,' I added.

My husband laughed. 'How she manages to give haircuts in that tiny corner of The Refuge I don't know!'

When we arrived at our destination we were singing softly together.

'Count your blessings, name them one by one,
Count your blessings, see what God has done.
Count your blessings, name them one by one,
And it will surprise you what the Lord has done.'

What did any passers-by think? It didn't matter. Everyone in Anderson was used to the pair of us!

It was nearly ten o'clock when we opened the door of The Refuge and went in, just on time for our Bible talk. One of the volunteers was giving it that night. He took a short piece of Scripture and explained what it meant to the men and boys who were present, and to the volunteers too. Questions followed on these occasions, often relating what had been said to personal circumstances. Sometimes lads would ask us to read verses that had been spoken about on other evenings. We would go over these with them word by word to help them remember. A good proportion of our young boys had difficulty reading. Some Bible Times were quiet affairs, especially if they followed news of the death of one of our regulars or if someone was ill or in trouble. We would be asked to pray about situations, and when that happened a hush settled on the room as we went into prayer, a hush broken only by the words of the prayer and quiet weeping. At times like that the barriers came down, and men and boys allowed themselves to cry. Hugh and I, along with the rest of the volunteers, were often overwhelmed by the weight of the tears we carried to the Lord in prayer.

We went again to the Mission, asking if we could have yet another member of staff. The workload had become impossible. Although a huge amount was done by our growing band of about eighty volunteers, there needed to be employed staff at each location to cover all eventualities. Hugh was not always available as he still did night patrol, visiting the men and women in Anderson's skippers with food and company and the opportunity to talk. But we did not go asking the Board to advertise for a worker, we went suggesting that Margaret Taylor be given the job. Of all people Margaret knew and understood the needs, and she better than any of us knew how to get alongside people. The Board accepted our recommendation, and she joined the team. Margaret has kindly agreed to have her testimony included in this book. It will warm readers' hearts.

God provided for us in some interesting ways. Our son, Paul, attends Jordanhill School, and the staff and pupils there have been most supportive of the work we are doing. At Christmas they have a collection to provide food parcels for homeless people. One Easter they asked me to attend their end of term service. I left it with over 300 large chocolate Easter eggs and cards to give to those who had no possibility of having one. What hurt me was the realisation that some of the children we met on the streets were still young enough to have been at home expecting dads and mums to buy Easter eggs for them. They were not much older than some of the pupils who had made the cards and given the eggs.

But then came a bombshell. The Refuge was threatened with closure. We had already been out of Cornerstone for a time while the building above it was demolished, and we didn't want to go through that again. With the Board and staff of Glasgow City Mission and our volunteer workers, Hugh and I carried the problem to the Lord in prayer.

9

Margaret's story

I was brought up in a room and kitchen in a tenement block in Glasgow's Gorbals. Although there were eight of us, Dad and Mum, my two older sisters and three younger brothers, I always felt alone and sometimes left out. Dad worked on the railway, it was steam trains then. My dad was often out, but Mum was always there for us. Summer nights are what I remember best, and wishing they would last for ever. My gran stayed in Govanhill, and we used to walk all the way to visit her. Mum would push the youngest in the pram and I would trail along behind her. It was a long walk.

In 1967 when I was eleven, we moved to a house in Torryglen. We thought it was like a castle, with a living room, four bedrooms, kitchen and bathroom. The bathroom was a real treat, though we had had an inside toilet in the Gorbals. Soon after moving there, I went to secondary school and it was there I met Chick. For the first time in my life I had something of my very own, my friend Chick. After school we walked up the road together. He was football daft, so we played together. I just loved being with Chick. He was everything to me.

At fifteen, I left school and went to work at the check-out in the local supermarket. Chick left too and he got a job with the cleansing department. That only lasted a week. It just wasn't for him. Then he found work as a painter and decorator. He loved that and did really well. We were very happy, and we even started saving up to get engaged.

One evening we arranged to go to the cinema. I was ready just after seven, but Chick didn't turn up until ten past ten. He had been to the pub for a couple of beers. I was so angry. I suppose I wanted all his attention and felt I wasn't getting it.

'It's all over between us,' I told him, when eventually he arrived. 'That's us finished.'

At first Chick didn't take me seriously, but I meant it. He made to leave the house.

'I'll walk you round the road,' I said, picking up the dog's leash. The dog came at the sound of it. We walked round the corner of the street.

'Don't let's finish like this,' Chick said. 'It's only an argument. Let's make up.'

But I wouldn't. I remember walking away. It was the first time we'd ever parted without speaking. I went home with a heavy heart and didn't sleep.

The next day was Saturday. I went into town and walked about the shops all day. Inside myself I just wanted to get back home and to see Chick again. I didn't like the feeling of us arguing and I was very unhappy. Eventually, tired and depressed, I went home. Dad was sitting in the living room looking very serious. I wondered what I'd done wrong.

'You'll need to go to the hospital,' he said. 'Chick's in hospital.'

I knew my boyfriend was to have played golf with his dad that morning and thought he'd fallen and broken his leg or something like that.

'I'm not going to see him,' I told Dad. 'We're not talking.'

My father looked up. 'You'll have to go.'

I put my coat on, still thinking Chick had had an accident. Dad took me to the hospital. As we went up in the lift I rehearsed what I was going to say, but it all went out of my head when we went into the ward. It was the Intensive Care Unit, and Chick was there, all wired up to different machines. I looked at him, his eyes were closed, he wasn't moving at all. My mind spun round, trying to figure out what was happening. I sat down beside him and stayed there, I've no idea how long for, till his parents came. I couldn't believe what was happening and I was sure that he was just going to waken up and smile at me.

All weekend we sat at his bedside. The hours dragged past and nothing happened.

'Come on and we'll go for a coffee,' Chick's mum said, about one o'clock the following Tuesday afternoon.

We walked round the corner to a cafe and sat there, Chick's parents and me. It seemed for ever that we were there then we walked back to the hospital. As we went into the Intensive Care Unit a Chinese doctor came to meet us. I knew something terrible had happened. They had turned the life support machine off. Chick was dead. He had died of a cerebral haemorrhage. My ears heard what was said, but my head and my heart couldn't take it in. I didn't believe he had gone.

What followed was terrible. I lay on the couch for days. The doctor came and gave me tablets to make me sleep and other tablets too. I went to the chapel to Chick's funeral. But I was so angry. I was angry with him for dying, angry with God for letting it happen, and angry with myself for falling out with Chick. I was so full of grief and anger, but I couldn't cry. I just sat there in a screwed up knot of hurt and anger and despair.

Two weeks later I heard that there were ways of talking to people who were dead. I was told that you could use a board with letters of the alphabet and an upturned glass, and that spirits would spell out messages to you. I don't want to give details of how this is done because nobody should ever do it. My sisters came into the room and watched what I was doing. I lit two candles and put the room light off. They were frightened, but for the first time since Chick died I had feelings inside me, I actually felt excited. I talked to the board and the glass spelled out messages. When I asked to speak to Chick, the glass spelled out that he wanted me to join him. My sisters stopped it then. They said it was ridiculous and that I had to start making plans for the future instead of living in the past.

That night I sat with Mum and Dad for a while before going to my room. In those days it was trendy to have your room furnished like a bedsit. When friends came in that's where we went, we didn't sit with our parents. That wouldn't have been done at all. My bed was right on the floor because I'd taken the legs off. That meant we could lounge around on it. When I went to my room that night, I took all the tablets the doctor had given me and hid the bottles. I don't know what happened then, but Mum told me that they heard a loud thump and found me on the floor. I was rushed to hospital and my stomach was pumped. I wasn't pleased to find I was still alive as I couldn't cope with the hurt and the pain inside me. I just didn't know how I could face each tomorrow. I wanted to go to Chick.

That went on for some months until my sister decided it had to stop. One night she took me to a bar and it was there I met C. C. was four years older than me and his friends were even older than him. Through them I found a way to escape from the pain that was consuming me. My new friends were all heroin users. The first time I tried it all the pain and the hurt and the emptiness and longing melted away. Within a week or two, at the age of 16, I was injecting heroin and it had become the most important thing in my whole life. I was hooked.

C. and I married when I was 18 and we split up when I was 19. Over the following 14 years I was in two relationships and that was when I had my three children. Caroline, my eldest, is my princess. David, who is in the middle, is a delight. And Damien, the youngest, is a delightful free spirit. My last partner was also an addict and I found myself in the situation of having to support two habits, his and mine, There was nothing I wouldn't do for heroin. And my partner, who was both physically and mentally abusive, had no qualms about how our drugs were earned. Addicts will do things they would never have dreamt possible. There is no need for me to describe those years, they hurt me too much and there is no reason why they should also hurt anyone reading my story.

It was during my relationship with him, and just after David was born in 1987, that I met the couple who were to be used to change my life. The first time I saw Hugh and Maureen McKenna they spoke to me, introduced themselves and told me about Jesus. I didn't want to know, I was quite sure Jesus couldn't help me.

'Would you like a cup of tea?' they asked.

'I don't drink tea, only coffee,' I replied cheekily, 'and I don't want to know about your Jesus.'

'What's your name?' enquired Hugh.

'Margaret,' I answered, looking defiantly at him. But the look in his eyes startled me. They were full of compassion. Although I didn't recognise it then, it was the compassion of the Lord.

After that I looked forward to meeting Hugh and Maureen. They knew my lifestyle, knew I was still injecting and that I was still doing the things addicts do to pay for their habit. But they still treated me with respect and assured me that they were praying for me. I was very cynical about what they believed but I couldn't deny the goodness of

143

what they were doing. What impressed me most was their consistency, their faithfulness in doing their work in the city streets regardless of the weather or the time of year.

But soon after Damien was born my life seemed to go to pieces. The Social Services told me that if I didn't get my act together and go into rehabilitation I would lose my children, they would be taken away from me. I loved Caroline, David and Damien and for them I went into rehabilitation for ten months. I got well physically and mentally and came out free of drugs. But inside I was proud and self-sufficient, just ripe for a fall. And it came. It was a Saturday when I arrived back from rehabilitation and by the Monday morning I was pumping my arm full of heroin. I knew quite well the road I was going down, I knew my kids would be taken into care, but the power of addiction ruled over everything. My rehabilitation had failed. My mental and physical problems had been dealt with, but I was left with the spiritual problem we all have and until it was addressed, drugs ruled.

The children were taken away from me. They went to stay with my partner's mother and sister and there is no way I can ever express my gratitude to them for caring for my children when I couldn't. Eventually I ended up in a hostel for the homeless and that was when I reach my lowest ebb. I became unwell and needed surgery, but before I could have it my drug habit had to be stabilised so I was given methadone to get me off of heroin. After my operation I went back to the hostel, but was warned that I would have to remain on a very strict maintenance programme as I had by then been using heroin for 21 years.

On Tuesday night, 27th November 1992, I was walking along Bath Street in Glasgow's city centre. Things Maureen and Hugh had said over the years flooded into my mind.

'I don't even know if you're up there,' I told God. 'But if you are, I need you, I need you to show me you're there.' That cry came from the bottom of my heart.

'Hello, Margaret,' a voice said. It was Cathy, a girl I'd met through the McKennas. We fell into step together.

'Where are you going?' I asked her.

'I'm on my way to the prayer meeting,' she told me. 'Want to come?'

I nodded. There were over a dozen there, many of them young, and most of them volunteers who worked with Hugh and Maureen. I was made to feel so welcome.

'Would you like to come to church on Sunday? Anne Marie, one of the volunteers asked. Ten of the prayer group members were to be baptised at the service.

'That would be nice,' I replied, but only because they had been so kind to me.

'You and Cathy could come on Saturday and stay overnight,' Anne Marie went on, 'then we could go to church together.'

When Saturday came, Anne Marie's door was opened to us by her son. He was about twelve, and he invited us in. I didn't want to go, but having come this far there was no way I could go back.

The following day we went to church and I watched as the ten young people were baptised. After the baptism, the minister asked if anyone wanted to give their heart to Jesus. I looked at Cathy and saw that her hand was up. I could never do that, I thought to myself, never. Then the minister's wife came and spoke to me.

'I'm so glad you gave your heart to Jesus,' she said warmly.

I looked. I had my hand up. Even then I knew that only God had made that happen, I certainly had not. If ever I think that I've done anything to contribute to being saved, I'll look back to that day and remember that I couldn't even raise my own hand. Even that had been done by Jesus.

Within days I made contact with the McKennas and they welcomed me as a sister. It was just then that Glasgow City Mission had acquired the premises for Cornerstone and work was about to begin on it. Maureen invited me to lend a hand. That invitation showed great wisdom. In those early days of faith, I needed to have my time full and I needed to be out of the madness of the hostel where everyone was either on drugs or drink. Early each morning I left the hostel, collected my methadone, and headed for Cornerstone. Along with Gregor, who has become a good friend, and other volunteers I *scraped and scrubbed and cleaned the dirt off.*

By January 1993 I had cut my methadone by half, to 50ml a day. The McKennas encouraged me, urging me to continue my access visits to the children every Tuesday afternoon. This meant travelling to Cranhill for the one hour visit. I hated the journey, I hated the involvement of the Social Work Department, but Maureen and Hugh helped me through that tough time. Then I had the struggle of getting out of the hostel. I was told that I would never be given a furnished flat in the west end of the city, but God knew better. Imagine how thrilled and thankful I was when the Housing Department got in touch to say that they had a furnished flat in the west end for me.

I went to Cornerstone every day. We cleaned and painted, and painted the cleaned bits then cleaned the painted bits! And when Cornerstone opened it was just thrilling to see the girls come off the street into the refuge it provided for them. By March I was off methadone completely. God took away all desire for drugs from my heart. For the first time in 21 years I was completely drug free. I no longer needed heroin to comfort me, I had found real comfort in the Lord Jesus, the comfort that comes from the forgiveness of sin. I couldn't understand then, and I still can't begin to take it in, that Jesus loved me when I didn't even like myself, that he accepted me when I was totally unacceptable even to myself.

My faith was soon to be tested. I had applied to

the courts to get Caroline, David and Damien back and the case was due to come up. Hugh and Maureen spent much time in prayer with me, and others did too. A volunteer, Janette, held a house group meeting in her home and one of the people who attended was an elderly lady called Mrs. Combes. Every week Janette told me that her group had been remembering me in prayer, and that Mrs. Combes was asking for me. I could hardly believe that God put it on people's hearts to pray for the likes of me. One day I had the privilege of meeting Mrs. Combes, when I went to the church she attends.

'That's her there,' Janette said, pointing to a very elderly lady, 'She'd love to meet you.'

I went to introduce myself.

'Hello,' I said. 'I'm Margaret Taylor.'

The old lady turned round to look at me and her eyes lit up.

'God is so good,' she said. 'I was just praying the other day and saying that I know it's not for us to know what happens to the people we pray for, but it would be nice to know. And here God has sent you to show me that my prayers are answered.'

Mrs. Combes is one very special lady.

The court case lasted for three days. I felt as if my life was being hung out to dry. All through the proceedings I prayed that God's will would be done, and that I would accept the result. On the third day, a Friday, the judge said that I would know the result shortly. As I left the building I felt sure that I would be given my children back, and I quite consciously trusted the whole business to God. Two weeks passed before my lawyer phoned, and it was with the news that I had lost the case but still had access rights. It was a sunny summer day, and my friend Anne Marie and I walked down to the River Clyde and had a picnic on the grass. I prayed, there and then, that God would help me to trust him, and he reminded me that he had plans for me, plans to give me a hope and a future.

Soon after that I was allocated a house in the west end. Friends helped me to clean and decorate it, and it became a haven for me and for others too. Caroline, who is now 20, is engaged to Mark, a lovely boy who is good to her. David is the British Junior Weightlifting Champion. And Damien, who is just growing up, has a very different mum from the one he used to have. I love my kids so much. God has given me such a love for them, and I have the indescribable privilege of them loving me despite all the years of my addiction and of them being away from me. I see Caroline nearly every day and the boys come to stay with me at weekends when they can. There is no way I can put into words what it means to me to have my children in my own home.

The Lord certainly has had plans for me and I am beginning to see them work out. I have just completed a Higher National Certificate in Counselling, which I could never have done without the support and encouragement of my Christian *friends. For some time I have been privileged to help with recovery groups in Barlinnie and Low Moss prisons. When I am there I present a three point recovery programme, involving physical, emotional and spiritual aspects. I know from my own experience that to treat the physical and emotional side of things at the expense of the spiritual is to miss out on the path to true recovery.*

How can I sum up being in the Lord's service? I see it as doing some of the things Jesus did 2000 years ago, when he went about doing practical and helpful things, showing people that they were worthwhile and worth listening to, sharing with them and speaking to them of his Father God. I thank God from the bottom of my heart that he bent down in love to me, rescuing me from the pit I was in and saving me to serve him by serving some of the neediest people in Glasgow. Hugh and Maureen are my spiritual parents, and I thank God for their love and care, their steadfastness and consistency. And I thank him also for Maureen's mum who always had an open door for me and an open ear.

It is my prayer that God will use the work we do so that others, people just like me, will be drawn to him and find forgiveness and loving acceptance. I love the Lord for who he is and for what he has done in calling me his child. And I still can't begin to take it in.

(Margaret began full time work with Open Door Trust in September 2000.)

10

The beginnings of change

It was a source of great sadness over our years of working with homeless people, to see the age of the men become ever younger, until we were seeing boys on the streets, young lads just in their early teens. They came to The Refuge for warmth and comfort and, I think, for the mothering they got there. For some of them it was the only mothering they had ever known. It worried us that these boys were crushed into The Refuge with men old enough to be their fathers and grandfathers, maybe even their great grandfathers. On a wet winter's night there could be a hundred there. Among our men were a few who were worldly wise in the worst way, and not beyond taking advantage of naive boys. We saw it as a priority to separate them for the good of the youngsters.

For some time the Council had been trying to close down The Refuge in order to demolish the building and make space for development. A meeting was arranged at which we were to be given the opportunity of discussing relocation. The day of the meeting was drawing closer when Hugh and I found ourselves pursuing our old hobby, peering through dirty windows into vacant premises. This time it was not a public house but a former newsagents and confectioner, and it was just a few yards along the road from The Refuge.

'Ever had the feeling you've been here before?' Hugh asked, as we wiped the window with a tissue to give us a better view inside.

I nodded.

'It's all the better not having a bar and pub type seating when it is for boys,' I said. 'We don't want anything that will make them feel more at home in that kind of atmosphere.'

Hugh agreed. 'And because it is so close we could send boys who arrive at The Refuge along here.'

We agreed that the premises had a lot going for them, but we rather heaved a sigh at the prospect of what all would need to be done before the door ever opened. We'd been there before three times, with The Rooms, Cornerstone and The Refuge, and some things don't get easier with practice.

Timothy Edwards, who was then Glasgow City Mission's Training and Development Officer, must have felt like hiding when he saw us coming. He knew us well, and realised that when we saw a need we were eager to try to meet it, and we didn't like hanging about. He listened to our case patiently.

'Some of these lads come from families of second generation drug abusers,' Hugh explained to him. 'We've got to accept that nowadays we are dealing with kids who see abuse as normal, kids who don't have to hide their habit at home because that's where they learned it. It's a bit like smoking was in the fifties.'

I listened to what Hugh said, knowing it was true, but still finding the words horrifying.

'And some of the boys who come to The Refuge regularly from hostels for the homeless have just left school.'

My husband is good at explaining things, and that is what he set out to do. 'You see,' he said, 'marriages and relationships break up so often that young folk sometimes find themselves with parents and step parents in three or four, even five, different places. There is a sense in which they are homeless because they don't actually have a home rather than having been put out. I can imagine a boy whose dad and mum are divorced, and for a while he lived between the two of them after both went into new relationships. But when these couples part, where do the kids go, dad or mum, step-dad, step-mum, or to granny, and if so, a real one or a step one? There is no end of the permutations we meet. You would almost need a piece of paper and a pencil to work them all out.'

Timothy looked thoughtful and sad.

'Then there are the boys who have been kicked out,' I didn't want them forgotten, 'boys who don't have jobs and aren't eligible for unemployment benefit. They fall between two stools, and some parents are quick enough to realise that the only way their lads will get any support is if they put them out. I've known boys whose folks have actually told them they were being put out for their own good, so that the Council would give them somewhere to stay!'

Timothy needed no more persuading. He did all the necessary paperwork and was a great help to us in getting this project off the ground.

The day came for our meeting with the Council officials at The Refuge. Several times before we had met with officials who had been sent to tell us that we had to leave our premises, that the block was due to be demolished, that there were plans for a fine new development. And each time that had happened we left the meeting with the promise of an alternative site. Would that happen again this time?

'The priority,' explained an official, 'is to get rid of these unsightly blocks and put up buildings that will be a credit to the city. That's what brings in business, and business brings money and money helps relieve poverty.'

Hugh doesn't get excited and raise his voice. He's very good at presenting an argument quietly.

'But our priority is to meet the needs of those who are poor today. They can't wait to reap the benefits of inner city regeneration. That's why we feel it is imperative that The Refuge remains open until we have somewhere else for the men to go.'

The officials were sympathetic, but adamant.

'I'm afraid crunch time has come,' one told us. 'You have to move on, and soon. Will you agree to being out in six months if we put it off till then?'

We didn't actually answer their question, instead I asked them one. I don't suppose they were surprised.

'There's an empty shop on the corner, the old newspaper place, could we have the use of it for the next six months?' Before they could answer, I had started to walk towards the building. They followed, and as we walked I told them about the problem of mixing hardened men with young boys. They had no choice but listen.

We arrived outside the shop.

'Even if we could only have it for six months it would be a help,' I told them, hoping that any arrangement would become long term and allow for the boys' work. 'For that length of time we could open it as a clothes store.'

I think I even surprised the Council officials with that suggestion, and they were used to me!

'We are given more second-hand and new clothes than you would ever believe,' I explained. 'People in churches all over the city save them for us and we distribute them to those in need. A clothes store would allow folk to come and chose what they require. It would meet a real need in this part of the city, and it leaves people with their dignity when they go into a store and chose for themselves.'

The men looked thoughtful, they seemed impressed by the volume of support we had, and the wide area from which it came. Hugh latched on to their interest.

'We couldn't function without the support of many hundreds of people,' he told them. 'We are given gifts of clothes, toys, food and much else besides.' He gave instances, Jordanhill School's Easter eggs, our city centre baker's cakes, the butcher who donated hundreds of sausages, Christmas boxes, not to mention thousands of man hours given voluntarily and sacrificially.

God worked a miracle. When the men left us outside The Refuge, we had a stay of execution for that building and a short term let on the shop.

I overheard one man say to the other as they left, 'Every time we come down here to tell them to move on they end up getting another place.'

We could hardly wait to get inside to give vent to our thanksgiving and praise.

For a few months we used the shop as a clothes store then prepared it for the boys. The decor was trendy, speakers were installed to pipe out their favourite music, and all it needed was a name. That's when I remembered a Mickey Rooney film from my youth. In it boys who were in need were sent to a place called Boystown. We didn't need to look any further for a name, Boystown it was. The lads claimed the place as their own as soon as it was opened, and it became a haven for them, somewhere they could get away from the pressures, the loneliness and violence, somewhere they could feel cared for, loved, fathered and mothered. It also reduced the mass in The Refuge and allowed our men to sit down rather than stand, and it meant that they could have their food served to them in a civilised manner. These things were important to us. We wanted to treat people with dignity, no matter what state they were in. They were made in the image of God, and it was our privilege to serve them and minister to them. Providing a pleasant atmosphere was part of our ministry.

Boystown was a wonderful place for us as well as for the lads. Various activities were started up, among them a lunch club and the inevitable football team. It was our interest in football that showed us how Boystown broke down barriers. In Glasgow, probably more than anywhere else outside of Ireland, there is a great divide between Catholic and Protestant young folk. They may not know much about their religion, but it colours their relationships with each other. This even extends to sport. Catholics support Celtic Football Team and Protestants follow Rangers. One of Rangers' officials invited the lads from Boystown to visit their stadium.

'Watch them separate,' our friend said quietly, as the boys went through the tunnel on to the pitch, Catholics to the right and Protestants to the left. And that's exactly what happened. But although the young folk separated as they went through the tunnel, they were all one in Boystown. Coming from our sectarian Glasgow background, that meant a great deal to us.

Having the boys on their own meant we could get alongside them individually, find out their backgrounds and their needs, and do what we could to meet them. We began to see new ways of developing that side of our work, and we found ourselves thinking how best we could take it forward. But by then we had three refuges open, medical services up and running, and our regular night patrol. On top of that a lot of my time was taken up speaking about the work at churches, schools and various other venues. That allowed us to make the work known quite widely, and I believe it helped people to understand and have compassion on those at the bottom of society's heap. I hope and pray it made those who heard these talks think twice about writing people off. The down side of it all was that we were working to an unsustainable schedule. Hugh and I were tired. It really made us think when a friend who worked in a similar field told us that people in the front line normally only did it for three years before moving on to less demanding areas of service. We were entering out tenth year, and though God had given us strength for every day, we were aware that perhaps the time had come for change.

As we spoke to the younger folk, we came under strong conviction that more had to be done for them, not just the management of their crises, but the kind of building up that takes time and effort, a lot of both. Had anyone come into the refuges they would have looked around and assessed them as successful, and so they were, but only in a short-term way for most of those who came to us. There were exceptions, of course, and each one of them thrilled us. However, we became more and more convinced that something more long-term had to be done.

It was at that critical time that we were offered a sabbatical and we were very grateful for it. Through the kind offices of a trust set up to help overseas missionaries to go home, or home missionaries to have a rest, we spent six weeks in Clearwater in Florida, resting, reflecting and praying. Paul was given leave of absence from school and supplied with a package to keep him up-to-date. It was one of my enjoyments of that time to do his schoolwork with him and to discover more about current trends in education. We were right on the coast, and after ten years spent on Glasgow's city streets, the water, the heat and the resting time were a benediction to us. We were especially grateful to have that time together as a family. Since babyhood Paul had seen us come and go at all kinds of odd hours, often returning in the middle of the night. Only because he was so content and had the stability of my mother living with us and caring for him were we able to do the work we did. Without my mother's support it would have been impossible. There are no words enough to thank her.

It was a very different McKenna family that returned to Scotland. Refreshed and rested, we were ready to face whatever the Lord had in store for us. Before we left, plans had been made for a temporary refuge in the Broomlielaw area of the city and work on that was well underway. That helped to confirm us in our belief that God was leading us in another direction, that of helping people to rebuild their broken lives. We knew we could not do both. After taking the counsel of wise friends and praying much about the matter, we were sure that as the Lord had led us into Glasgow City Mission, he was now leading us out, and we had to follow him. When we discussed it with Paul, he was right behind us, even though he realised that we were managers with the Mission and that leaving would be a step of faith in financial terms. In October 1997, we tendered our resignations with a leaving date two months later. This was a traumatic time for us, but it was God's time. We were both fifty, had we left it longer we would have been too old to begin a new work and establish it.

Although I never doubted God's ability to do the work, I sometimes doubted mine, especially in the early hours of the morning. Many times I woke up feeling anxious and fearful about what the future held. Hugh's steadfastness was a great support to me when I voiced my doubts. But when God calls, peace only comes in answering and following. The Lord used his Word to assure us we were doing the right thing. 'Praise to the God and Father of the Lord Jesus Christ, the Father of compassion and the God of all comfort, who comforts us in all our troubles, so that we can comfort those in any trouble with the comfort we ourselves have received from God' (2 Cor. 1:3-4) spoke to our hearts. On 12th December 1997 we began a new adventure, a new journey. Full of hope at the opportunities, we embarked on our new challenge.

11

The birth of Open
Door Trust Glasgow

Sometimes God's Word becomes amazingly alive,
and that's what happened to Hugh and me at the
beginning of our new work. 'Now to him who is
able to do immeasurably more than all we ask or
imagine, according to his power that is at work
within us, to him be glory in the church and in
Christ Jesus throughout all generations, for ever
and ever, Amen!' (Eph. 3:20). The account that
follows is a glorious example of that verse.

'Mum,' asked Paul, a few days before we
finished working with Glasgow City Mission,
'what will we do now you won't have a car through
your work.'

'I don't know, Son,' I replied honestly. 'But
God will give us everything we need.'

His question made us think, but we didn't have
to think for long.

'What are you doing about transport for your
work?' a friend from St. George's Tron Church,
the congregation of which we were members, asked
us a few days later.

'We haven't really worked out things like that,'
Hugh admitted.

Our friend nodded his head. 'I'd like you both to go to the car saleroom and choose a car that would fit all your needs.'

How wonderfully God opened his children's hearts to respond to the needs of his work. We did as our friend said, and left the saleroom with a second hand Honda Civic. Our new work had transport!

St. George's Tron Church has many gifted members, among them at that time was Laspic Stewart, a solicitor. Hugh and I met with him in his office and he helped us to set up the Trust. But a trust needs a name. We puzzled over that and we prayed about it. One day, after we had discussed it to the point of exhaustion in Laspic's office, we decided to call a halt and apply ourselves to it together the following day.

'What exactly do you want the Trust to be known for?' Laspic asked, as we left his office. 'Simply stated, what are your aims and intentions?'

'We want it to be a trust God will use to open doors to many people, an open trust that will never turn anyone away.'

'How about Open Door Trust then?' suggested Laspic.

Hugh and I looked at each other. That was it! We met the next day to work things out. The name Open Door Trust had been used before, but we marked it out as different by calling it Open Door Trust Glasgow. We were recognised as a Scottish Charity in January 1998.

Laspic's help was invaluable. He saw to the formation of the Trust and its registration as a charity, things that we could not have undertaken ourselves. The original trustees were Hugh, Laspic and myself. Within weeks of its foundation, a friend, who is now one of our trustees, phoned.

'Do you have accommodation?' he asked Hugh.

'No,' my husband told him. We've not got anywhere yet.'

'I'm involved with Glasgow Radio Fellowship,' our friend explained, 'and I think there might be a room in our office that you could have the use of. Are you interested?'

Hugh assured him that he was very interested and arranged for a meeting at the premises. We were stunned when we looked out of one of the Fellowship's windows.

'Look,' I said, 'look at the view down there.'

Hugh came over to the window. Underneath us was a recently demolished site, the same site that had once housed Cornerstone, The Refuge and Boystown. We stood there together, praying that one day God would provide another building in that area of Glasgow, somewhere with its doors wide open to welcome those in need and to support them as they tried to find their feet again. By the end of that visit we had an office. Things were moving.

However, our office was just for administration purposes, and we didn't anticipate it being central to the practical work we intended to do. We still had to find a place in which we could prepare food for our night patrols, transport to take it round the streets, and also decide exactly where our patrols would cover. God knew our needs and he answered them in a remarkable way. The minister and Kirk Session of St. Vincent Street Free Church allowed us to use their premises to prepare food. Hugh's mum and a friend gave the soup and food containers that were required by law, no longer could we go round with a flask and tinfoil wrapped sandwiches. A Daihatsu van big enough to carry all our equipment was made available to us each night. It was rather like Cinderella, it had to be back by dawn. Then came the decision about where to patrol. We were convinced of the importance of remaining in the same area and not losing contact with the many needy people there who had become our friends over the years. God seemed to be propelling us forward at speed.

The official launch took place on 31st January 1998 in our church halls. By then we had five trustees, all godly and gifted men, and Hugh became the Trust's Director. Over 200 people attended the launch, many of them we had known for years and a good number were our faithful supporters and volunteers. It was a day to remember. God even used that occasion to further equip us with a typewriter, second-hand computer, office desk, chairs and other things we needed as well as financial support. The Trust was founded and launched, it was time for the work to begin.

Our first night patrol was on a bitterly cold Monday a week or so later. Hugh and I met with some volunteers and, after a time of prayer, went out on the streets. It felt as though the clock had been turned back 11 years. It was tempting to wonder why things had happened like this, and I found myself doing just that. But, when our homeless, hurting and needy friends gathered around the van we both experienced a real sense of freedom and peace. Our hearts began to soar as we saw how God had brought this about. We were humbled by the friendship and the concern of the people on the street. An excitement took us over. We were up and running. Other projects were soon underway, including a lunch club for men, women and children, and recovery groups, both in prison and outside of it, through which we hoped to give people the backup they needed to enable them to step away from addiction and homelessness and poverty.

We had previously had a work in Barlinnie Prison, now we took it up again. I will always remember how I felt the first day I heard the prison door clank shut behind me. The loneliness and alienation nearly overwhelmed me. And if I reacted profoundly when I was there on a visit, how did young men feel when they knew they were there to stay? We had prayed for a long time about the possibility of working with young addicts inside prison. It seemed to us that the time to reach these lads was when they were inside, and hopefully off drugs, rather than when they came out and started using them again. Amazingly, four of the first prison group of ten were boys we'd worked with on the streets.

Treats are non existent in prison, so the Mars Bars we took ensured our popularity. But seeing the men and boys eat them really moved me, they were like kids having a Saturday treat. There was real pathos there. All of those we worked with were there for drug related offences, most for theft committed to support their habit. One surprising discovery was the frustration, and often the sadness, the prison warders felt when these young men joined the revolving door syndrome. They were no sooner out of prison than they were in on remand again, having re-offended almost immediately to obtain the drugs they craved.

The drug recovery groups were hard work, very demanding. We had to give our all for the two hours we were there. And the boys we met through them needed follow-up when they got out. That was our vision, our goal, as we recognised that there was little point in doing frontline work unless there was backup support. The first thing Hugh offered to do for them was to meet them on release. It is hard to believe, but it is true, that as men leave prison there are pushers waiting in the car park ready to suck them back into their world. Many were grateful to Hugh for getting them past that first temptation and hurdle. Recovery groups were also established outside of prison to provide ongoing support in a safe and unthreatening atmosphere. We knew this work would be difficult, and it is, but it never ceases to amaze me what a bowl of soup, a roll and sausage and a motherly hug can achieve. What many lads needed was a mother or father figure, and that is what we and our volunteers made ourselves available to be.

A month after our new work started, we had a phone call from Rev Jackie Ross of Blythswood Trust, a charity which collects clothes, furniture, medical supplies etc. from all over Scotland, runs charity shops in this country, and distributes aid in Eastern Europe. We had obtained furniture from them on many occasions for families in need. Jackie arranged to come and see us. His visit was memorable, as we discussed how we might work together. Before leaving, he invited us to visit Deephaven, Blythswood's centre in Ross-shire. Our visit to him was even more memorable. Iain Macdougall, who is one of our trustees, Hugh and I drove through a blizzard to get there. But what a welcome! Deephaven is a vast hanger, and as Jackie showed us round he introduced us to the volunteer workers. In Deephaven donations of every kind are processed and prepared either for sale or distribution here or for transporting overseas. We found much to inspire us.

Over our working years in Glasgow we have met many people in need of material things: mothers who, with their children, have been thrown out of their homes possessing only what they were wearing at the time, and occasionally that was only nightclothes, homeless young folk, old men dressed nearly in rags. It is easy to assume that they should be grateful for whatever they are given and to hand over a plastic refuse bag of clothes. But we believe very strongly that whatever people's situations are they should be treated with dignity, with the same care, courtesy and sensitivity as we would treat a member of our family. Regardless of our circumstances we are all made in the image of God and that gives us dignity and worth. One of the Trust's aims was to open a clothes store where people could choose what they wanted and needed, where they could accept freely but with dignity. Blythswood's operations helped us see that our dream could become a reality.

The time came for us to brave the elements and head back to Glasgow. But Jackie wasn't finished with us.

'Could the Trust make use of an old double decker bus?' he enquired, indicating one that was sitting nearby.

I laughed. 'What would we do with that?' I asked.

He turned in the direction of the vehicle. 'Come and have a look.'

We followed him.

This was no ordinary bus. The downstairs was equipped with a cooker, fridge, sink, tables and chairs, and the back was fitted out as a children's play area. Upstairs was a counselling area. My heart leapt, and when I looked at my husband, I knew what he was thinking. Could we use an old double decker bus? We most certainly could.

For once in my life I was speechless!

'Think of taking the bus out on night patrol,' Hugh said. I had. 'We could prepare the food right on site and serve it from the bus.' Hugh nodded to the stairs. 'And we could use the upper deck when people wanted to talk privately or if anyone needed a place of safety.'

I found my voice again.

'Could we really have this?' I asked Jackie. 'It would be an amazing asset to our work.'

He laughed. 'I'm offering it to you. But there is just one problem.'

Iain, Hugh and I looked at him. 'You'd need to find a bus driver,' he said. 'Do you know anyone with a Public Service Vehicle licence?'

My mind zipped back 24 years, to my bus driving days in Cumbernauld. I'd not driven a bus since, but I still had my licence. This is why I drove buses, I said to my Lord, this is why!

'I have a PSV licence,' I told Jackie. I could see Hugh smirking by my side.

'You!'

I told him the story, and how I had often wondered about that little episode in my life. I wouldn't wonder about it again. Nearly quarter of a century ago God had this day in mind, and he was preparing me for it. I couldn't wait to tell Mum!

A few weeks later Jackie Ross drove the bus

from Ross-shire to Glasgow. By then it had been serviced, passed its MOT test, been painted white and decorated with Open Door Trust Glasgow's logo. 'The Big White Bus' is now well known in Anderson. It reaches out to over 150 homeless and needy people on the streets. We serve over 200 rolls and sausages as well as sandwiches, tray bakes and fresh fruit each night. Sadly even women and children are regular visitors to out bus. The Lord had fitted another piece of his jigsaw in place and we were enjoying finding out what the picture would turn out to be.

In the course of the Trust's first year it became apparent that we needed a large reliable vehicle of our own. The Trustees prayed about this, believing that the Lord is able to supply all the needs of his people. How he supplied ours was nothing short of miraculous. Just at that time one of our regular supporters, who lives on the opposite side of the world, was moved to send a gift, and his gift was enough to buy a Madza van, exactly the kind of vehicle we needed. The Trustees who had met in prayer met again, this time to thank and praise the Lord for his miraculous provision.

Because Hugh and I did not see ourselves primarily as administrators we were thrilled when he provided willing volunteers, gifted in office administration, bookkeeping, banking and all the other things that needed to be done. The Trust owes a great debt of gratitude to Julie and Suzanne who man the office. Nor did we view the Trust as a two man (person!) operation, very far from it. Faithful volunteers were involved in all aspects of the work, helping at the lunch club, on the streets, in recovery groups. Without them the work could not be done.

That was an exciting year, but it was also a very sad one. My brother John became ill and showed no signs of recovery. Investigations revealed a malignant tumour pressing on his heart and lungs. It was inoperable. John was given just a short time to live. Susan and their three boys, Jonathan, Ian and Terry, were wonderful with John, but it broke my heart to see what they were going through. John and I had been very close as children, but although we always remained friends, that closeness had gone with the years. However, over the last months of his life God restored it to us, a gift I will always treasure. The Trust's splendid volunteers stepped in, enabling me to make myself available to the family over those months.

Many times we had talked with John about the Lord, but he had never taken much interest. He respected us and what we believed, but it was not for him. In the last months of his life my brother and I talked often about God and about heaven, and he often asked me to pray for him and with him. But, although I knew his interest was deepening, I could see him fading away and still without a faith that would take him into the arms of the Saviour. Eventually the time came when he needed the care only a hospice could provide, and by then he was so poorly that just close family members were able to visit. But one day a friend of his managed to get in without being stopped and I thank God he did. This man had faced huge problems in his life, and a short time before someone had told him about Jesus, and he had found the answer to his needs in this world and beyond in the Lord. He shared this with my brother, and was used of my heavenly Father to bring John to faith. What joy there was in my heart when John told me that evening that he had put his trust in Jesus and that he was soon to go home to heaven. It was very soon. John lapsed in and out of consciousness for the next few days then went to be with the Lord.

1998 began with the founding of Open Door Trust Glasgow. It ended with John's home-going. There was a beginning and an ending, and the Lord was with us throughout.

12

Rebuilding broken lives

Glasgow entered the new millennium with the unenviable reputation of being one of the six poorest European cities, and things are getting worse. Homelessness, poverty and drug misuse are all on the increase, casting an ever darkening shadow over the city. 1999 saw the worst ever drug related death toll in greater Glasgow, 148 deaths. These are only the tip of the iceberg. Nearly every death leaves a grieving family; parents without a child, children without a parent. And those who leave no-one to mourn them present, perhaps, the saddest of all, the poor folk who have lost touch with their dear ones and who were mourned for years before they died.

The majority of the Trust's workers have had between ten and twenty years experience of working with needy people. Over that time they have earned the respect of the people we serve and friendships have grown. What is just as important, perhaps even more so, is that we have respect for those whom we serve, often they are battling against life in a most heroic way, and none more so than young mothers.

One of the problems about poverty is that all a poor person can look forward to is more poverty and increasing debt. In Open Door Trust Glasgow we aim to give our friends things to look forward to, things we take for granted but which are beyond the wildest dreams of the poorest people in the city. In 1999 we hired a bus and used it to take about 35 children on a farm visit. It was a delight to see them among horses and ponies, cows and sheep, lambs and rabbits. But what touched my heart was their mothers' faces. Free of the city, free of responsibility, free of the weight of working out how much the day would cost, they looked like children themselves.

From the farm we headed to Largs on the Ayrshire coast and a meal there. Seven of the children were due to start school and, thanks to a generous donation, we were able to take them to a shoe shop and buy them each a pair of shoes. Many of these children never get decent shoes, and rarely get new ones. The delight on their faces took me right back to McAslin Street, to the first Sunday of each May and my new black patent shoes. I knew what they were feeling, I could remember it. Just before these children went to school, the Trust was able to help provide uniforms too. In the year 2000, 30 pairs of shoes were bought for children starting school. In just one year that aspect of our work has grown more than fourfold.

Rosie's story
Rosy is the eldest of six children, but very small.
The first time I met her, she was waiting outside

a supermarket. When her mother, Liz, came out, it was with a pitifully small amount of shopping and a very sad and harassed expression. She was really struggling. Liz, who had a hard time with her husband and was often down to her last penny and in debt to feed her children, came to our lunch club as soon as she was invited and we have got to know her and the children well.

When our seven little ones were due to start primary school, Rosie was about to move into secondary. Despite her mother's best efforts, and she did do her best, Rosie was going to start poorly dressed and with very tatty footwear. That day in Largs we were able to buy shoes for Rosie, a kind volunteer provided some good underwear and school clothes. Had she started her new school dressed as she was she would have been picked on right away. As it was, she turned up as smartly dressed as the others. It is in such simple and practical ways that the Trust seeks to ease mothers' burdens.

At school children learn about Christmas, they have parties, make cards and a great build up of excitement begins. They see Christmas in the shops from October onwards, tinsel and gift wrap, selection boxes and expensive toys. And on the television too, they are bombarded with advertisements about what they could ask Santa to bring. It is hard to imagine what it is like in our consumer society for those boys and girls whose circumstances are such that, after all the months of hype about Christmas, on the day itself nothing happens. We do our best to ensure that is not the case for the children we know.

Churches, schools and individuals from all over the city donate toys and gifts to the Trust. Food parcels are packed with treats as well as necessities, and family sized sacks are filled with toys, all to be distributed to our friends. In 1999 financial donations allowed us to take our children to the pantomime, and what a thrill that was. Having been told we were coming, the cast called out a welcome to the children from Open Door Trust. Their wee faces shone, they were famous for an evening. St. Vincent Street Free Church provided a Christmas dinner for the mothers and children. St George's Tron Church, which gives us the use of their premises every Wednesday for our lunch clubs for over 130 men, women and children, also hosted a Christmas dinner for all our friends at which we distributed food parcels and presents. The older children in Jordanhill School kindly wrap them all. At that time of year we remember God's gift of his own Son, the Lord Jesus Christ, to be our Saviour. That makes us want to celebrate, and we want to help others celebrate too.

The Trust has been able to send some of our older children to Scripture Union Camps. There they have had the holiday of a lifetime, abseiling, canoeing, eating midnight feasts, playing team games, just being the children they are. One of the sad things about poverty is that it makes old men and women out of young boys and girls. That means that their memories of childhood are memories of adult worries and concerns. So many of the people we meet in the streets have few happy childhood memories. We try to ensure that our youngsters are given treats to remember. Of course, at Scripture Union Camps the children learn about the Christian faith, and about the saving love of the Lord Jesus. The Trust can give them some happy memories to store away for the future, but only God can change their futures. It is our hope and our prayer that they will find their futures in him, safe and secure in the arms of Jesus.

Over and over again we have been shown the importance of giving children happy things to remember. When I think back to McAslin Street, I thank God for good memories. Sure, there were terrible things going on just as there are in Glasgow's streets today, but there were good things too. Although Dad sometimes suffered from severe depression, a depression that cast a gloom over our home for long periods of time, I also remember happy times with him. I remember Sunday afternoons at the piano, and it was probably the only piano in the street, when Dad played Scottish songs and some classical music too. He had a fine voice and he and I sang our way through our Scottish heritage. Those were special times. And I remember Mum's pride in my brothers and myself, her hard work to make sure we were well turned out and well fed, and the exciting time we had each year, she and I, when we went to buy my new black patent leather shoes. How proud I felt as I carried that shoe box home. Those were good times. The memories the Trust can give a child will be different from mine, but I hope and pray that they will give them the same pleasure.

We believe that Open Door Trust Glasgow is unique in the package of services it offers, from shoes to pantomimes to food boxes, from lunch clubs to farm visits, from night patrols in Glasgow to the West Highland Way, from visits to poor homes to drug recovery groups in prisons, and much more besides.

The Big White Bus is often the first link in the chain. That is where we meet with homeless people, women and girls on the streets, and drug addicts and alcoholics in need of food and acceptance. To our great grief we are meeting today the children of some of those we first met on night patrol over a decade ago. Some children of prostitutes are now on the streets themselves, and the same is true of our early addicts and homeless people. That saddens our hearts, but it also inspires us to do what we can to break that appalling cycle.

Often we meet a young addict on the street, then we meet in prison, then on the street again. Prisons have revolving doors for drug addicts, they are no sooner out than they are in again, having offended to feed their habit. We work in Barlinnie and Low Moss Prisons, holding drug recovery groups in both, where we work together with the Social Work

Department, community services and addiction services. The Trust aims to provide a holistic approach to the problems we meet there, covering the physical, emotional and spiritual areas of life. To do less than that is to reach out with incomplete help to incomplete people.

Our physical activity programme provides support in physical recovery and great fun too. It covers everything from football to a walk of about 100 miles along the West Highland Way, an arduous trek through the Scottish countryside. That walk worked a miracle in the lives of the boys and girls the Trust took there. For three of the five days the sun shone and the countryside looked beautiful. They enjoyed themselves thoroughly, sharing the challenge and the fun of it all. Days four and five were different. It poured. Having built friendships in the sunshine, they supported each other in the rain. When one slid in the mud, the others helped him up again. When the rain and damp made sleep difficult, they chatted the night away to keep each other company. At the beginning of the walk they were individuals facing a challenge, by the end of it they had gelled into a group which had met the challenge and overcome.

That trek along the West Highland Way is a good picture of the Trust's work. We are as delighted as our friends when they are enjoying the sunshine of release from addiction or homelessness or prostitution or poverty, and we hope to be there for them, and that they will be there for each other when the sun stops shining, when life throws challenges at them, when they need support. A great deal of encouragement is given to our young people to become involved in helping others, and we guide them to a variety of voluntary work. Some help in collecting clothes and other donations from churches, others give assistance in the stores and in food distribution to those who are homeless. So many of them when we first meet have lost all dignity, they begin to find it again as they help us help others.

And they begin to find themselves. The Trust offers support on that voyage of self discovery. Many of our young people carry burdens of poverty and abuse, going right back to their earliest years. To wallpaper over their problems would be to conceal them for today and save them up for tomorrow. Our support groups offer a safe environment in which they can explore these issues and begin to learn to deal with them. That kind of support is long term, which is what we felt we lacked in the work we did before the establishment of the Trust. We were on the front line meeting crisis situations, but to fail to address the underlying problems just helps someone until the next crisis comes along. Vast sums of money are spent meeting crises and so little in preventing them. Government after government, council after council, pours money into solving crises, usually after a public outcry about addicts dying on the streets, or young people living in cardboard cities.

Our former minister, Rev. Eric Alexander, said, 'a desperate situation should never be answered with a desperate measure'. How true that is.

The Trust is now well established, and we thank God for that. We have three employees, Vic Walker, Margaret Taylor and Hugh, and we thank God for them. However, one of the things we have come to realise is that we have a need to consolidate our work and to base it on one site. At present we are using borrowed buildings in various parts of central Glasgow. We are so thankful to those who lend their premises and to God for moving their hearts to do so, without them we could not have begun our work, but we have a vision for the future, and we believe it is God who has given it. We see our work set in one building, somewhere in the same part of Glasgow. That will enable us to offer a comprehensive range of services which we are already planning for and praying about.

Glasgow's problems are not confined to the city centre. Every area has its needs, and every area has its church. One of our aims is to provide training facilities which congregations could use to enable them to meet the needs in their own areas. Already we are invited out to do training courses, but it would be a much more effective use of time and resources if we could provide them centrally. We would be able to use the experience and expertise of those who have been freed from homelessness, addiction and prostitution, poverty and homelessness, to train others to reach out in love. Since Anne Kelly's daughter came to us on placement, we have had many such students. Having a suitable building would allow for the development of the placement programme.

Of course, if people from a long distance away wished to use our services we would go to them. This has already happened. Rev Iain MacAskill, Free Church minister in South Uist, has a work there with alcoholics. He invited Hugh and myself, Laspic Stewart and Margaret Taylor to visit him there. God blessed that visit in a heartwarming way as we shared with the people there about our work and our lives. Margaret could hardly take in the openness of an island welcome, and the islanders were receptive to her amazing testimony. The sun shone for our four days on South Uist, despite it being January, but as we sat in the sunshine waiting for our plane back to Glasgow, we heard that it was fogbound there. Our young folk in the city benefited by the delay. As we waited for the plane, Iain introduced us to the delights of South Uist curry pies. We enjoyed them so much that we took two dozen back with us!

A building in the city centre would be a place to which mothers and their children could have daily access, where creche facilities would be provided so allowing mothers the freedom to pursue interests they can only dream about now. And there would also be a place for children. Great numbers of disadvantaged children lose out on their education. It is not that they are less able, it may be that they don't have shoes and can't go to school, or that their parents are addicts and they fall behind because they have no sound sleep and nowhere quiet to do their homework, or that they are being abused and their fears make concentration impossible, or that they have early morning and late evening jobs. The Trust hopes that these young people could be catered for in a building, could be taught and brought up to a standard at which they would cope with mainstream school again. But our building is still in the future, and only if it is God's will. Hugh reminds me often that our work is not dependent on a building, and that it is the work which is important. I just have to look at the lives that have been changed to know that for sure.

Open Door Trust Glasgow can only function because of its many wonderful volunteers. They give their time and energy and resources in a very sacrificial way. The work is exhausting physically, emotionally and spiritually and the Trust needs to have a care for them too. In the spring of 2000, a group of us went on retreat together to a beautiful highland estate. There we rested and relaxed, talked and prayed. That kind of break has become a necessity and will be repeated. We give thanks to our friends Ronald and Christine for this wonderful provision, and for the support and love they give to our friends.

Gregor's story
Gregor's background was hard, he had never

really had a childhood. As a result he was a very damaged young man when we met him, without any spark of hope or ambition. Not long before we acquired Cornerstone, Gregor broke free of his addiction by the grace and mercy of God, and he was then at the stage of needing his mind and his hours fully occupied to distract him from the temptation to return to his old way of living. With Margaret and other volunteers, he spent weeks getting Cornerstone ready for use. Gregor proved his worth as a worker and we had no hesitation in recommending him when he told us he was being interviewed for a job. We know his employer and he has no regrets. He saw the lad's potential and had the courage and good sense to take him on. He has a valued employee to show for it. Because of the problems our young friend faced in his early childhood, he has had to rethink and rebuild right from the beginning. He has come a very long way, and he has a long way still to go.

We have a theory based on all the years we have worked with addicts, both alcoholics and drug users, that when they are helped to break free of their addiction, they are terrific workers and very keen to please. However, we are aware that not all employers are like the man Gregor works for, not all are prepared to take on board people with troubled backgrounds. That is why we aim in the Trust to find employment for our young folk, or at least to give them work experience on which a prospective employer could make an assessment of potential. But before they are able for employment out of our supported structure, we intend to employ some for a time ourselves in the work of helping others who still are where they have been.

There is no way we can ever thank God enough for what he has done for us, though we thank him over and over again every day of our lives. And we are quite overwhelmed by the way in which our Lord has chosen to use our experience of the rough side of life to reach out to others who are where we were. Many have challenged us, many have troubled us and many have given us real cause for joy.

Karen's story
We first met Karen about 14 years ago, and she completely refused to talk to us. Only after knowing her for five years did the wall start to crumble and we began to speak to each other. Eventually Karen came to Cornerstone and she also came to Christ. What a thrill it was for me to see her with Margaret and to know that their lives had been changed and a new future lay ahead for them. After she became a Christian, Karen decided to be baptised and she asked me to stand beside her at the service. She had written out her testimony in order to read it to the congregation. But she was only able to say four

words before her voice broke and she handed me the sheet to read for her. But her four words would have been enough. Before she was overwhelmed by the wonder of it all, Karen told the congregation, 'I just love Jesus'.

Some time later Hugh and I were at a garden party and Karen went with us. We had been asked to speak about the work of the Trust. It was a splendid affair, and it was there I got a taste for fresh salmon! As we mingled with the crowd a dear Christian friend took Karen under her wing. Our friend's love and compassion put Karen thoroughly at ease. She told me afterwards, 'That women didn't even know me, but I still knew she cared.' The person who cares most of all for Karen is the Lord Jesus Christ, and they are now in each others company for ever and ever. Karen died in the summer of 2000.

I suppose it is because I am a woman that I see our work in very domestic terms. It seems to me that the vision we have for the Trust is that it should be rather like an automatic washing machine with its various cycles. It starts with the pre-wash, goes on to the main wash, is rinsed over and over again then comes out clean and ready for use. That is our prayer for those we meet, that they are prepared by God to be freed from their addictions and problems, that they are washed clean through Jesus Christ, then supported by the Trust until they are fit and ready for use wherever God will lead them.

And it may be because I'm a mother that I look at the young people I meet on the street and think of our son Paul. He has enjoyed a security and comfort that most of these lads and girls have never known, but through our work he is fully aware of the sad side of Glasgow. I am grateful for that, because I don't think he'll ever see people in trouble and assume it is all their own fault. Through Paul, I think a little of that message has reached his fellow pupils at school too. And it is only when the mindset changes that says that if you are on the streets it is because you deserve to be, that society will get its act together and treat the root causes of poverty, addiction, prostitution and homelessness. In the mean time Open Door Trust Glasgow and other Christian agencies will reach out to those in need with the love of Jesus, and many others will do the same from decent human kindness.

When I was a girl I used to start at the bottom of the stairs and work my way up. To do them well I had to brush away all the dirt and dust, scrub them thoroughly, then apply the whitewash. When I did that they gleamed. I would stand at the top, underneath the huge skylight, and look down the stairwell with pride. Occasionally, just occasionally, I cut corners and missed out on washing the stairs. When I did that there were streaks on the whitewash and no satisfaction.

In my mind I'm still whitewashing stairs and the whole of the Trust is in it with me. We are starting at the bottom with boys and girls, men and women, and we watch them, encouraging them, supporting them as they climb the stairs. We see some of them giving up along the way for the climb and the cleaning is hard work. But some climb on. We watch their struggles as they teeter on some steps and we try to be right behind them, but some fall. Yet others go on. More effort is needed the higher they climb and some tire, but the Trust tries to be there with reassurance and practical support. The higher our dear friends climb the better we see them in the brightness of the skylight window *and the more clearly we see the Lord's hand in it all*. And some have reached the very top landing and have stepped out into the light, the Light of the World, our lovely and loving Lord Jesus Christ.

We are still working on the foundation of the ministry. We are only at the beginning, there is much to do. Some people ask what our success rate is. My answer is that it depends on what you class as success. For us success is when we see someone beginning to smile again, someone looking forward to being part of tomorrow. It is when fear and sorrow melt from faces and confidence starts to take its place. Success is when a disadvantaged young person who has dreams and ambitions for the future is helped to achieve them. And how is this success achieved? It is always and only through the grace of the Lord Jesus Christ, through his love and compassion flooding hearts and lives that were hungry and thirsty for them.

If you require any information regarding **Open Door Trust Glasgow** then please contact 342 Argyle Street, Glasgow, G2 8LY. Tel: 0141 243 2336

Christian Focus Publications publishes biblically-accurate books for adults and children. The books in the adult range are published in three imprints.

Christian Heritage contains classic writings from the past.

Christian Focus contains popular works including biographies, commentaries, doctrine, and Christian living.

Mentor focuses on books written at a level suitable for Bible College and seminary students, pastors, and others; the imprint includes commentaries, doctrinal studies, examination of current issues, and church history.

For a free catalogue of all out titles, please write to
Christian Focus Publications,
Geanies House, Fearn, Ross-shire,
Scotland, Great Britain, IV20 1TW.

For details of our titles visit us on our web site
http://www.christianfocus.com